TEACH US TO PRAY

TEACH US TO PRAY

Edited by
Tom A. Jones
and
Sheila Jones

ILLUMINATION PUBLISHERS

Teach Us to Pray: Daily Power Series.
© 2023 by Illumination Publishers International. Previously published by Discipleship Publications International in 1995.

Cover design: Toney C. Mulhollan.
Interior Layout: Chris Costello and Nora Robbins.

ISBN: 978-1-958723-07-4.

Edited by Tom A. and Sheila Jones. Sheila passed from this life in 2022. Tom Jones now makes his home in the city of Tuscaloosa, Alabama where he has helped start a new church planting. Some of Tom A Jones' other books include *No One Like Him, Deep Convictions, One Another, The Baptized Life, Glory in the Church, Mind Change, Mind Change Moments, The Kingdom of God, Volumes 1-3, The Prideful Soul's Guide to Humility* and many others.

Illumination Publishers International
www.ipibooks.com

Dedication

*To those often
unnoticed disciples who
are physically limited but
who mightily affect the
world with the prayers that
they pray. They are not
unnoticed by God.*

Contents

The Needs We Bring

The Difference It Makes

Introduction

Prayer at the Center

When the disciples said to Jesus, as recorded in Luke 11:1, "Lord, teach us to pray," for once they were asking for the right thing. Prayer is powerful, and there is nothing we need to know more about than prayer. If a relationship with God is the most important matter in life, then nothing is more important than knowing how to pray.

A disciple of Jesus who does not know how to pray is like an athlete who does not know about eating properly or an accountant who does not know how to use a calculator or a parent who does not know how to show love. Anyone who tries to take up his cross and follow Jesus and does not learn how to pray is like a towing company that tries to move stalled cars with bicycles and ropes. If we rely on nothing but human power, the life Jesus calls us to is impossible. On his own, not even the most stable, most healthy, most intelligent and most determined person can do it. Only as we are intimately connected with God through prayer will we continually find the forgiveness, strength, inspiration and direction needed to live the life Jesus described and expected of his followers.

Prayer is not the only thing needed by disciples. It is just *the most important thing.* It is not the only thing needed to accomplish our world mission and build great relationships and have great families. It is just the most important thing for those of us with these goals. For this reason, prayer must not be seen as one more piece of the Christian pie. It must be at the center of all the other pieces. It must not show up as you see it in figure 1 but rather as you see it in figure 2.

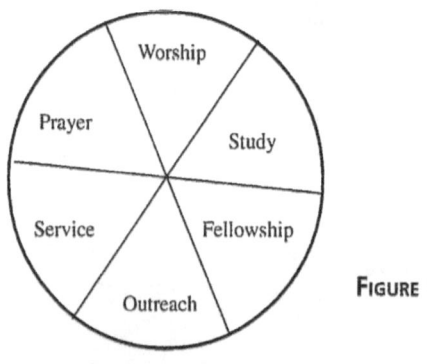

FIGURE 1

FIGURE 2

There is a major difference in these two ways of thinking. When prayer is at the center, the influence and power of God will show up in everything. When prayer is just one of a list of things we do, we greatly diminish its potency.

Finding God, Not Just Getting Answers

Often we pray because we want answers. God certainly answers prayer, but we must not pray just to get an answer. Maybe that is one of the things God is teaching us when he doesn't always give us exactly what we want. God does answer prayer, but we must pray in order to know God and walk with him. As Jesus' disciples who have taken on his mission, we are concerned about getting the gospel to the entire world, but we must not pray just so we can finish that mission. We will not finish it without prayer, that is for sure; and it is one of the reasons we are writing this book at this time. But as we pray, we must be seeking more than even a righteous conquest of the world. We must be seeking God. We must be seeking his heart. We must be seeking to have his character. If we come to prayer with that attitude, we will be about the mission, and we will find the power to complete it because we will find God himself.

Richer and More Effective

Try as we may, we will never be fully prepared to write a book on prayer. By the time some of you are settling in to read this material, many of the authors will have learned something else and will wish they could have an opportunity for some revision. But God in his graciousness uses imperfect people and imperfect thinking to advance his perfect purposes. As much as we are able, we will base what we write here on the absolutely reliable words of Scripture. We are confident that God, through his Spirit, can take this unchanging truth, blend it with our changing experiences and understanding, and bring it to your heart so that your prayer life can become richer and more effective than ever before. This will not be the last word on prayer, but we have prayed that it will help all who read it (1) to put prayer at the very center of their lives and (2) to make prayer the heart of a dynamic relationship with God and never a powerless religious routine.

So Much to Learn

Most everyone who reads this book will in some way already know how to pray. It is not as though this is first time you have ever thought about doing it. It is very likely you have read several books about it. For some years or months you have been getting up every morning and finding time for it. You not only pray alone, but you pray with others. *But no matter how long you have been doing it, you still need to come to Jesus Christ and say, "Lord, teach me to pray."*

When the disciples first came to Jesus with their request, I am confident they already had prayed many prayers. But when they saw him in prayer and saw the difference it made in his life, they recognized that they had much to learn.

After you have finished this book, our hope and prayer is that you will be encouraged and inspired. I believe those who embrace what is written here, will walk more closely with God and be used more powerfully by him. But even if you read every word, praying as you read, and strive with all your heart to live it, you will need to keep praying, "Lord, teach me to pray," because there will still be so much more to learn.

I am amazed at some of the most basic types of computer software I work with. After using a leading word processing program for five years, I was still discovering new things I could do with it. Now I am using something newer and far more sophisticated. The amazing thing is that it will most certainly become outdated and be replaced by our systems manager long before I figure out all the ways I could be using it. If there is this kind of potential in something designed by mere men, how should we think about prayer?

God wants to work powerfully in our lives. He will teach us if we are eager to learn. Many of us are deeply thankful for what we have already been taught. We can see much fruit from what we already understand. But how much more is there for us to learn? Given that prayer is as big as God himself, shouldn't "Lord, teach us to pray" become our never-ending plea?

Watch Out

As you read what follows, take each chapter seriously. Listen carefully to Scripture and to committed disciples who are seeking more of God, and get ready to explore some new and exciting spiritual frontiers. Take a few minutes to write down what you think you most need to learn about prayer. Then get ready to learn not only that but other things you had no idea you needed to know.

Prayer can change us. Prayer can change the world. If thousands of disciples use this book and pray with more knowledge, more faith, more consistency and more honesty than ever before, watch out! Nothing will be the same. Much needs to happen in us and in our world, and it all starts with prayer. So we come to God and say, "Lord, teach us to pray."

T.A.J.

THE
GOD WHO
HEARS

*Approaching God with a clear
understanding of who he is and his
commitment to us*

1
God Almighty

RON DRABOT
Charlotte, North Carolina

> This is what the LORD says—Israel's King and Redeemer, the LORD Almighty: I am the first and I am the last; apart from me there is no God. Who then is like me? Let him proclaim it. Let him declare and lay out before me what has happened since I established my ancient people, and what is yet to come—yes, let him foretell what will come. Do not tremble, do not be afraid. Did I not proclaim this and foretell it long ago? You are my witnesses. Is there any God besides me? No, there is no other Rock; I know not one (Isaiah 44:6-8).

Upon entering the full-time ministry at the age of 23 in Columbus, Ohio, I quickly realized that leading, maintaining and growing a spiritual ministry was much beyond what I humanly could accomplish. A mighty deed such as this required direct help from an Almighty God. Knowing little as to how I would achieve this "first shot" at success, I decided to pray all night outside my apartment in hopes that the Almighty might help me solve this dilemma.

God is the Almighty God. There is nothing he cannot do. There is no victory he cannot win. There is no tragedy he cannot overcome. No mountain he cannot move. I was determined to know this Almighty God better than I knew anybody. I realized that though I might not be as talented as others in the ministry, I could be one of God's closest friends. I committed myself to a radical relationship with him. We would talk more. I would read more. We would dream together, laugh together and cry together. I decided to spend at least four hours a day in my walk with God, often beginning at 4:00 a.m. The victories I have experienced since that day can all be traced back to a decision to guard carefully my time with the Almighty God who can do what I cannot do.

The Sovereign God

Eight years into our marriage, Lavonia and I saw God work in ways that showed he is indeed the Sovereign Lord. We were told by doctors that we had little chance of being parents and were told by one doctor that it would take the intervention of God for us to have a child. After four years of praying and after developing the conviction that God could not only could give us a child, but give us twins as well, Lavonia became pregnant. The evidence was in: The Almighty God had been working overtime, and she was going to have not one baby but two! The fact that they were fraternal twins made God's miracle all the more amazing.

But joy quickly turned to grief as Joshua, our firstborn, died just 17 days after his birth. It was testing time. Time for a gut check and a heart analysis. Could I still trust through all the tears? Would I still obey his every last word though we had lost our first child? Would I accept the good but not the difficult? Could I respond just like Job? (Job 1:20-22).

We claimed the fact that God was still at work. Still struggling with our loss, we prayed for more growth in our Johannesburg, South Africa, church than ever before. We decided Joshua's life and death and our godly response to both would inspire and convict many. People would still be able to see the Almighty God do his mighty deeds even in the midst of tragedy. During the next two months, we saw record numbers of people come to the Lord—people who will one day enjoy heaven forever with Joshua.

The Mountain Mover

After Joshua's death, we moved back to the United States and assumed responsibility for a 1500-member church in Chicago and six other Midwest churches, and I came face to face with a mountain called mononucleosis. I was sick for more than a year. The illness forced me to pace myself and depend much more on God through prayer. In our first calendar year, the church grew by more than 400. The Almighty God had once again defended his title.

In July and October of 1994, we experienced two of the most fruitful months in the 11-year history of the church. "What happened?" "How did you do that?" "Give us the recipe!" "Whisper the secret." We simply decided to pray more, and God did more. It is no coincidence that during both months the entire staff participated in a "prayer chain" that continued 24 hours a day, seven days a week for the entire month. We vowed to take "extra time" with God individually as well. Most of the men prayed a minimum of three hours a day in July! We also fasted throughout the month and prayed all night every night with each staff member choosing one night to call upon the Almighty. The more we prayed, the more God answered. We gave our attention to prayer and God gave his attention to us and performed mighty deeds among us. 1994 was a record year in terms of growth for the Chicago church, while at the same time, many leaders and other disciples were sent out to help other churches.

Never doubt that God is the Almighty and that there is none like him. Whatever your role in the kingdom, the Almighty God hears your prayers. He is not confined to small boxes and humanistic limitations. He is not a faraway God or one who stopped doing great deeds when the Bible's pages stopped being written. He is the same God today as he was then. To find him and see him display his mighty deeds, join me, and begin paying much more attention to prayer, and watch the God of miracles revolutionize your faith and make you fall on your knees shouting, "My God Almighty!"

Prayer

Almighty God, teach me to be content in every situation, no matter how overwhelming life might seem to be. I realize you have given me everything I need for life and godliness.

The thought of continuing my relationship with you for eternity in heaven fills me with awe and anticipation of that great day. I can only dream and wait in joyful expectation. Walking with you, God, on a daily basis is the greatest privilege I could have ever asked for. Please, God, continue to make me realize your constant working in my life. Please increase my faith so that I still trust, obey and commit to you whatever you require of me.

I know you will give me whatever I ask or imagine as I delight myself in you. I love you with all my heart and I desire to please you more and more. Thanks for being my comforter, best friend and awesome God. You have my heart, life, mind and soul. Use me for your purpose and for your glory.

Today I come before you with adoration, respect and humility for I realize that I, the created, am speaking with the One and Only Creator. Thank you, Father, for always being there even when I feel like you're far away, for it is those times I'm sure you're the closest. I truly believe that though I may dream, imagine, plan and hope, it is you who directs my path and leads me. I know that your ways are not my ways and your thoughts are not my thoughts. Help me always to be mindful of your power, love, compassion and acceptance of me as your adopted and chosen son. When life seems confusing, lonely and difficult, help me to focus on the cross. Help me to see the good in all situations, to use them for your glory and to be personally strengthened in my inner being. And help me, God, to always trust in your Almighty nature.

Almighty God, I love you and need you with all my heart. I commit this day and the rest of my life to you and your kingdom. In the great name of your Son, Jesus, I pray.

For Further Study:

Job 38
Psalm 139
Psalm 2:1-6

2
Abba, Father

Tom A. Jones
Tuscaloosa, Alabama

For you did not receive a spirit that makes you a slave again to fear, but you received the Spirit of sonship. And by him we cry, "Abba, Father" (Romans 8:15).

God is amazing. He can shine enough light through a small window to illuminate a whole house. In three small New Testament verses he opens up for us a whole new way of understanding him and the kind of relationship we can enjoy with him now and forever. First, we have Jesus in the Garden of Gethsemane, saying *"Abba, Father, everything is possible for you. Take this cup from me. Yet not what I will, but what you will"* (Mark 14:36). Then we have Paul, in Romans 8:15 (above) and in Galatians 4:6, saying that those of us who have come into Christ can also cry *"Abba,* Father." Once we understand the background of these verses, we will begin to understand something truly remarkable.

A Little History of the Word

To get the picture, we need a little help from the scholars. In the Greek New Testament we have here the occurrence of an untranslated Aramaic word: *Abba.* As the language spoken in everyday Palestinian life, Aramaic was undoubtedly used by Jesus for most of his teaching. Normally, the gospel writers translated what he said into Greek. But for a very special reason, Mark did not completely do this in chapter 14. In telling of Jesus' passionate prayer in the garden, he lets us know that the word Jesus used for God was *Abba.*

The closest you could get to that word in Greek was *pater,* which was the word for "father." To make sure he was communicating clearly, Mark includes both words in this passage, and so we get *"Abba*, Father." Most likely Jesus originally would have said, *"Abba"* or the more plaintive, *"Abba, Abba,"* and Mark gives us both the original and the translation.

However, here is the extraordinary thing about this little word: Research has shown that prior to Jesus it was never used as a reference to God. Indeed to have done so would have been considered disrespectful at best and blasphemous at worst. But Why? you may ask. Because this was a word used in the very intimate settings of family life. It was often the first word a baby spoke. It was something akin to the expression "Da-Da" in English. It was the word the little toddler used every day to refer warmly and affectionately to his father.

In a moving story, in *Raising Awesome Kids in Troubled Times,* Sam Laing relates how his three-year-old daughter was trying to get his attention while he was immersed in work, by saying from behind the door, over and over, "I'm out here, Daddy. I'm out here, Daddy." Had she been a first-century Jewish child, she would have said, "I'm out here, Abba. I'm out here, Abba."

As we have already seen, God is the Almighty. No human mind can grasp his greatness and power. It is right for us to behold his majesty and stand in awe. And yet what we learn in Jesus, the supreme revelation of God, is that we can know God as a little child knows his daddy. We can, amazingly, come to him with the same familiarity and the same confidence.

A Scandalous Idea

Before Jesus, no one dared suggest such a relationship. It would have been scandalous to imply that you could be on such personal terms with God and that there was so little distance between the two of you. But speaking in Aramaic, Jesus probably used this word in most of the cases where he spoke of God, teaching his disciples that they too could know God in exactly this way. (Why else would the word have shown up 30 years later in letters like Romans and Galatians, written to churches where virtually no one spoke Aramaic?)

Before Jesus, there was no one who could tell us what he could tell us about God. There was no one who had been with the Father as he had. But from intimate personal experience, he could assure us of the kind of relationship we could enjoy.

It would be a great mistake to focus only on this concept to the neglect of others, but once we get the whole picture, we should still think of God fundamentally as *Abba*—as "Daddy," as "Dad," as "Papa," or whatever the family word is in our cultural background. Even when our own home life was lacking, we must see God as the fulfillment of all a loving parent is supposed to be.

A Surpise Ending

The day this book was to go to the printer, I was doing a final read-through and found that the material I originally had written to conclude this segment seemed to fall flat. It was early in the morning. No one was up, and I plunged in, thinking it would only take me a few minutes to knock out something that was much better. Two hours later, I was still typing and cutting and typing again and starting to feel considerable frustration. I shared with my wife that I had "writer's block" and was going to have to just put it all aside for a while. Within minutes of leaving my computer and starting a quiet time, I was pierced with conviction. I had violated my own principle. Prayer had not been at the center of my efforts. I had written (or tried to write) without prayer, without confessing to my Father that I could not do it without him. No wonder I was having such a struggle. I was embarrassed. How could I be so foolish?

But here is the great thing: When I went before God to admit my failure, I did not find the Greek Zeus, ready to hurl down thunderbolts, or the Great Stoic Stone Face staring at me impassively. I found my Dad who disciplines me for my own good and forgives me freely when I repent. I could feel him shaking his head at my forgetfulness, but I could also feel his loving arms around me as I poured out my confession. "As a father has compassion on his children, so the LORD has compassion on those who fear him; for he knows how we are formed, he remembers that we are dust" (Psalm 103:13-14).

I am grateful to God for showing us through Jesus that when we pray, it is to our Dad.

Prayer

My Father, my Abba, in heaven, how incredible that I can approach you on such familiar terms. How unbelievable that I, a weak and sinful man who understands so little in comparison with all there is to know, can walk right in and talk with you as a little child would talk with his dad.

My Father, help me overcome the fears I have about pouring out my soul to you, about getting emotional with you. Help me to deeply understand that you want to laugh with me and to cry with me. Help me understand that I can totally trust you with all I am. Father, others may let me down, but I am thankful that it is impossible for you to do that.

Father, I know I must not take this for granted. Such a privilege was purchased for me at a high price. Without Jesus' atonement, my sin would forever keep me away from the warmth of fellowship with you.

Father, help me always to be humbled by this relationship, but, at the same time, to be empowered by it. What a tragedy it would be to have access to all your riches, but to live as though nothing amazing has happened. May all who know me see abundant evidence that I am your son and your are my Father. Use me to help others learn your real name. Through Jesus I pray. Amen.

FOR FURTHER STUDY:

Matthew 7:7-11
Matthew 11:25
Luke 15:20-22

3
Savior and Redeemer

MARILYN KRIETE

Save me, O God,
    for the waters have come up to my neck.
I sink in the miry depths,
    where there is no foothold (Psalm 69:1-2).

My Sorrow

The words of this Psalm, memorized months earlier in case of
"future need," raced through my mind with desperate intensity. My
needy time was NOW; David's words came to life along with the
thoughts that were flooding my mind. "You know my folly, O God;
my guilt is not hidden from you..." (vs. 5). Sin and guilt assaulted my
heart. "I have come into the deep waters; the floods engulf me" (vs. 2b).

The day was March 5, 1994. My birthday. The day after my
"mountaintop experience of a lifetime": the ascent of that ancient
giant of Africa, Mount Kilimanjaro. We had made it—Henry and I,
and the rest of our African ministry discipleship group. God was truly
with us! We had beaten the odds—we had challenged the giant and
won!

But my heart wasn't singing. Instead, an endless litany of
reproach and shame took hold of my mind and refused to let go. My
sins paraded before me. *Pride:* What else was it that had pushed me
to make it all the way? Did I ever push myself to please God with
equal intensity? *Selfishness:* Did I really care whether the others
succeeded? Mike obviously did; as eight of us staggered our way up
to the highest summit, he had stopped us to wait for the weariest. "All
for one and one for all." Why didn't I think like that? What kind of

a friend, a wife—what kind of a disciple was I? *Greed:* I'd been deluded to think of myself as a "generous" person, when the only things I gladly shared were things I didn't need! I'd watched a brother's ears grow red with cold, and held on to both of my hats. "I came prepared," was my thought, trying to justify myself. But in what does God delight—the "prepared" withholder or the selfless giver?

My leadership came up next for relentless inspection. I thought about Fatiel, our mountain guide over the past five days. He seemed to epitomize true servanthood; he led the way in humble service, arriving first but always putting himself last. He bent himself to the needs of our group, showing sensitivity to each of us individually. He made sure we all experienced personal victories—without taking credit for anything. I could write a book on his leadership—and he was not even a disciple! Was my leadership based on anything other than a self-deceived self-service? My heart sunk deeper into the miry pit of condemnation and despair, as ever-darker thoughts sprang to mind.

"My sins have overtaken me, and I cannot see. They outnumber the hairs of my head" (Psalm 40:12). I had been a disciple, a leader in the full-time ministry for more than a decade! How could God see anything good in me! Everything about me and in me screamed "Sinner!" and "Failure!"—surely God's grace had reached its limit for me.

Times like this hit all of us. We study, we pray, we share our faith. We see ourselves growing, really changing to be like Jesus. God blesses us with fruit, and our friends commend us. It is well with our souls... Suddenly, deep crevices of sin are exposed in our hearts, and the walls of well-being crack and cave in. Our sinfulness looms larger than life—larger, it seems, than the blood of Jesus can ever conquer. Tidal waves of doubt assail us. He saved me once from all my sins. Can he do it again? Will he? If I'm so blind to my own sinfulness, will he also be blind to my need? What can I expect when I, like the Pharisees, commit the very sins I preach against? We have glimpsed our true selves, naked and untouched by grace—and have forgotten the heart and power of our Redeemer.

My Savior

The Cross is enough! Then, now and always.

> Therefore he is able to save completely those who come to God through him, because he always lives to intercede for them...He sacrificed for their sins once for all when he offered himself (Hebrews 7:25, 27b).

Consider: "He is able to save completely": The lifeline he throws me is never too short, weak or worn out to pull me all the way in. "He always lives": He is prepared to keep on rescuing me until the day I die! "Once for all": One death was sufficient for all my sins, for all time! Jesus' grace isn't given with an expiration date, nor does it come with a clause to cover only the sins I am aware of. The sacrifice of his perfect, holy and sinless body was more than enough to satisfy God's wrath against ALL my sins—past, present and future! I need only to hold on to my confidence and hope in his promises (Hebrews 3:6,14; 6:19; 10:23).

God wants his children to be absolutely confident that we can draw near to him with freedom and assurance whenever we pray. Whether we are rejoicing in his blessings or crying in the darkness of our sins—he is near. He has brought us near. The cross is enough!

My Song

Back to March 5, the mountain, and my tortured thoughts: I remembered David's appeal to God as he battled with his own mountain of sin:

> But I pray to you, O Lord, in the time of your favor; in your great love, O God, answer me with your sure salvation (Psalm 69:13).

Without seeing the cross, David understood his Savior and Redeemer, and he knew that his only hope—his certain hope—rested in God's grace. "Now is the time of God's favor, now is the day of salvation" (2 Corinthians 6:2). I, too, could turn to God again and be certain of his salvation. God had shown me my heart and my everlasting need for forgiveness; he also showed me his heart and the everlasting nature of his grace. The pit had been slimy—but the peak of God's favor was back in sight!

Prayer

Heavenly Father, sometimes I feel like a beggar, coming to you in filthy rags of sin. But I know that in your grace and mercy, you welcome me, not as a beggar, but as your special child.

Thank you for the blood of Jesus, for his perfect sacrifice for me. Thank you that his death paid the price for all my sins, so that I can pray to you so freely through him. It's so humbling and amazing to realize that you see me as holy, blameless and pure because you've clothed me with Christ. I'm so grateful that I don't have to do "penance" or punish myself for my sins, because I know I could never do enough. Thank you that Jesus did everything for me!

Father, I think of the high priests who could enter your Holy of Holies only once a year, and only then with the blood of animals. I think of Esther, who fasted and prayed for the king to extend his golden scepter, so that she would be accepted and not killed for seeking his favor.

You've made the way so easy for me! Help me to pray boldly and confidently today, with great faith, and to never take your incredible grace for granted. Please help me to hate my sins and to really repent from my heart. May your Spirit fill me with love and peace and joy today as I seek to serve you. Thank you for Jesus, my Savior, Redeemer and Friend. In his name I pray, Amen.

For Further Study:

Isaiah 54:7-10
Isaiah 61:10; 63:1-9
Hebrews 4:14-16

4
Strength and Shield

The Lord is my strength and my shield;
   my heart trusts in him, and I am helped.
My heart leaps for joy
   and I will give thanks to him in song (Psalm 28:7).

Let me take you to the place where human imagination collapses. A short tour of the universe. The *Reader's Digest* version.

Twinkle, Twinkle

On the fourth day of creation God breathed 100 billion trillion stars into existence. Our own star, the sun, is just one of them. And a rather average one at that. For example, the star, Antares, is 27 million times bigger. Another 50,000 times brighter!

No doubt, these facts are difficult to grasp. Even more staggering when we realize every single star is different in splendor from each other. So different that God has given each one its own special name.

When scientists discovered the galaxy M87 several years ago, (one of countless billions, I might add), it was much easier to call it M87 than to give it and its cluster of 10 trillion stars different names. But not too hard for God. The universe is so large and the distances so vast that we measure it, not in miles, but in light years—the distance light travels in a single year. At approximately 186,000 miles per second, that means 6 trillion miles in one year. Did you know the closest star to our solar system is 3.5 light years or 21 trillion miles away? Driving at 55 mph, it would take more than 43 million years just to arrive. Put another way, if we could reduce the size of our sun to the dot over this letter "i," the nearest star using the same scale, would be 10 miles away. Stretching end to end, the visible universe is about 15 billion by 6 trillion miles across! And yet, in a profound understatement, the Bible only says, "He also made the stars" (Genesis 1:16).

The more that we appreciate the majesty of outer space, the more we appreciate Jesus. He is the Source, Center and End of it all. The same Jesus who nursed at Mary's breast and spoke of mustard seeds, is the One who spoke M87 into existence. Not in six days, not even in one day, but in the "time" it takes to say one sentence.

Truly God is strong. But David said much more than "God is strong." He said, again and again, "God is my strength." All of this awesome power of God was focused on meeting the needs of David.

All This Strength for Me

God's love is the application of God-power to the caring, protecting and sustaining of his children. Jesus is the supreme proof of this. He was the incarnation of the Living God (Isaiah 9:6-7). The en-flesh-ment of LOVE. In Christ, we learn to trust in God's ability to meet our daily needs.

Consider these examples in the life of Jesus:

There was a time when God was on his knees, washing the feet of his betrayer. So perfect was his love for Judas, that after three years none of the other apostles even suspected Judas. Jesus touched a leper when he could have healed him with a word. He stopped an entire parade to cure one blind man. He felt the gentle but desperate touch of a suffering woman despite the crush of the crowds. He cried over Jerusalem while others marveled at the buildings.

He openly wept at Lazarus' grave—even when about to raise him from the dead. After raising Jairus' daughter from the dead, he still cared about her hungry tummy. He was so approachable, a sinful woman felt confident enough to burst into a room of Pharisees to wash his feet. He could fall asleep in a raging storm because he exhausted himself serving others. Jesus changed a tax collector's name to "gift of God." He chose to speak of a God who would seek, weep, run and die for his children.

On the night of his betryal, he went out of his way to encourage his apostles knowing that in a few hours they would abandon him. He could have given Peter away with one cocked eyebrow but chose instead to protect his friend. Despite Peter's fierce denial, Jesus left him the keys to the kingdom.

He promised paradise to a thief who moments earlier was abusing him. Pushing on his nailed feet, he endured a few more seconds of agony just to reassure him with the words, "I tell you the truth." The cross is the epitome and glory of all God's strength and love in one event. An event offered to us all.

This is the love within disciples. A love that surrounds us with "songs of deliverance," a love that watches over us, nourishes and protects us. We are the apple of God's eye, his beloved children, carved on the palms of his hands and enveloped by a fiery jealousy (Zechariah 2:5; 8:2). This is the strength that shields us.

Because of Africa

I believe this because of what I have seen in Africa. We did not even know where Lagos, Nigeria, was until we were 35,000 feet in the air. We were only planning to be in Africa for three months. Five-and-a-half years later, I can say God has shielded my family in countless creative and unseen ways. We have had typhoid, malaria and severe dysentery. An exotic insect laid eggs deep in my son's skin, causing an allergic reaction. Someone tried to run Marilyn over with a car, forcing her into a jagged ditch.

We have lived in a city rocked by riots, choked by corruption and disintegrating before our eyes. We have been threatened by individuals and by a group of neo-Nazis. I have been followed by a deranged man, fallen into an open sewer, been bitten by someone, and vomited so hard I lacerated my throat. Two guns have been stuck in my face; I've been robbed in the house at knifepoint... And yet, we are, happy, thankful, in love with the mission field and only slightly dysfunctional. Our God is our strength and our shield.

Prayer

Father in Heaven, I praise your awesome power and your faithful love. Dear God, when my son Daniel was born, a new kind of love awakened within me—a different kind of love. A parent-child, father-son love.

I have often sat on the end of my son's bed and watched him while he sleeps, dreaming about things we will do together and what he will become. I know, Father, that similarly you watch me in my sleep and protect me and consider all the things that we will do together. I know that you have hopes and dreams for me, and I am grateful and amazed.

In the morning, whether my son awakens me or finds me at work in my office, I am thrilled when he first wakes and wants to be near me. I can now more easily imagine your joy when I awake and you are the first thing on my mind as I scramble to spend time with you.

All that I have and am I give to my son. I do dozens and even hundreds of things for him without his knowledge. I think and pray about his character, education and future wife. I carry him on my shoulders in busy markets. I look both ways when we cross the street because sometimes he forgets. I will do anything to care for his needs. He is my son and I am his abba. So too with you, O God, except your strength, your love and your wisdom are boundless…like the universe.

For Further Study:

Genesis 1-2
Zechariah 2
John 10:1-18

5
The God Who Enjoys

ROBYN WILLIAMS
Orange, California

> Moreover, when God gives any man wealth and possessions, and enables him to enjoy them, to accept his lot and be happy in his work—this is a gift of God. He seldom reflects on the days of his life, because God keeps him occupied with gladness of heart (Ecclesiastes 5:19-20).

Have you ever finished a project and taken a few minutes to admire your work? Even something as simple as vacuuming a rug can give you a sense of accomplishment. A report completed by deadline, a three-pointer scored, an A on a test or a clean house gives us enjoyment. These "daily" achievements bring us joy but do not compare to the wonder, awe and majesty of bringing a new baby into the world. I will never forget the feeling when we first brought home each of our children from the hospital. I could have sat for hours just holding them and staring at them. To me they were so beautiful, wonders to behold.

Now imagine the incredible feeling God must have experienced when he first viewed his own creation. He looked out over his world and saw the majestic mountains, the brilliant sun, the mighty oceans, the largest and the smallest of all creatures, and he saw that it was good. And then, after creating man and woman, he saw that it was very good. What a feeling that must have been! God enjoyed his creation! And, he continued to enjoy it. He enjoyed developing the nation of Israel into a beautiful bride (Ezekiel 16:1-14). He joyously sang through angels when his Son was born (Luke 2:8-14). He verbalized his pleasure in his Son through a voice from heaven on the day he was baptized (Luke 3:22). He ushered in his church with a powerful celebration on Pentecost (Acts 2). God knows how to enjoy life!

How would it affect your prayer life if you had a deep conviction that God enjoys his relationship with you? You may sometimes feel you are a bother to God, a frustration to him or a source of disappointment, but if you are seeking him and eager to find him, you—warts and all—are a joy to him, and your prayers come up before him like golden bowls of sweet-smelling incense (Revelation 5:8). He made you for a relationship with him, and he loves it when that relationship is real.

God Enjoys Talking to Us

The number of books God included in the Bible is evidence enough that God loves to talk to us. We all know how special it is to have one-on-one time with someone we love. Jesus spent that kind of time with God for 40 days and nights in the desert before being tempted by Satan. If you were on a deserted island for 40 days with just your Bible and God, would you be happy? If you find yourself thinking it would be boring or lonely, my challenge to you is to get to know God on a deeper, more emotional level. If you were close to your Father, you would know that such an opportunity would be the thrill of a lifetime. With God as your guide, partner and protector, you could explore something new every day; first, the island, then the oceans, then the heavens! God wants our relationship with him to be real and exciting.

To truly know him, we must absorb his Word. We must enjoy his talking to us. God's Word was written with one purpose in mind—to communicate his love. How easily do you recall the promises of love God has made to you?

- He promises to carry our burdens (Matthew 11:28).
- If we tithe, he promises to give us so many blessings that we will not have enough room for them (Malachi 3:10).
- He will grant you sleep (Psalm 127:2).
- We will have all we need (2 Corinthians 9:8).
- He will give us more than we can ask or imagine (Ephesians 3:20).

- He will meet all of our needs (Philippians 4:19).
- He will make everything work together for the good (Romans 8:28).
- Our children have angels to represent them before God (Matthew 18:10).
- All disciples have angels to serve them (Hebrews 1:14).
- Chariots of fire and angels are standing guard all around us (2 King 6:17).

And, this is just the beginning! God enjoys communicating his love to you through his Word. Do you enjoy hearing him?

God Enjoys Hearing Us Talk to Him

For there to be a relationship, both people must communicate. God speaks to us through his Word; we speak to God through our prayers. As we open up our hearts and thoughts to him in prayer, God enjoys hearing our prayers. We must let God know us through our prayers. Early in my relationship with my husband, Bruce, there were times he had to pull things out of me. But as our relationship matured, I began to volunteer my feelings and thoughts. The more secure I felt in his love for me, the more I let him know the real me. This is how our relationship with God should be.

The longer we are in the Lord, the more secure and real we should be in our prayers. King David was very real with God. On any given day, he could be very down or fearful or sorrowful or joyful. Whatever he was feeling, he communicated to God. As David revealed his heart to God, God was able to disciple him and help him to be "the man after God's own heart." Do you enjoy the fact that you can be totally real with God?

God Enjoys Watching Us

When watching our children play soccer, sing in a play, read the Bible, or baptize a schoolmate, Bruce and I have felt great joy. God also enjoys watching his children. God enjoys watching us share our faith. Recently, it was a joy to baptize a friend named Kathy into

Christ. She has changed from a shy, suspicious person into a loving, trusting woman of God. God rejoiced along with us as she began her new life in Christ.

As we become more like God, we will enjoy him more and more. Don't ever forget, though, that when we are humble and obedient toward him, we are truly a joy to him.

Today when you pray, understand that God enjoys having you in his kingdom and enjoys having you come to him as a son or a daughter. Rejoice in the relationship you have with him and commit yourself to give God even more joy by living to please him.

Prayer

Dear Lord, I thank you for wanting to know me. Thank you for revealing your love for me through your Word and your Son. I am so grateful for my present relationship with you, and yet I long to know you better and better. I pray that every day I will grow stronger in you, become more like you, and do more for you. Please help me be humble and see my need for you daily.

Help me never to neglect my time with you, to make it special, and never take it for granted. I, like Paul, want to know your Son in his sufferings and his resurrection.

I want to be a joy to you in all areas: as a wife, mother, daughter, leader, sister and friend. With you, God, I know all things are possible, so I thank you for the enjoyment of success even before it happens. Help me to see the chariots of fire and angels you have around me helping me be successful. Help me to enjoy all things as you do. I love you with all my heart. Thank you for loving me and enjoying me. In Jesus' name, Amen.

For Further Study:

Psalm 55
Psalm 100
Zephaniah 3:17

THE
HEART THAT
FINDS

Understanding how the spiritual condition
of our hearts makes all the difference
in our relationship with the Father and the kind of
response we will get to prayer

6
Hungry and Thirsty

G. Steve Kinnard
New York City, New York

> As a doe longs for running streams,
> so longs my soul for you, my God.
>
> My soul thirsts for God, the God of life;
> when shall I go to see the face of God?
> (Psalm 42:1-2, The Jerusalem Bible)

True prayer is a yearning for God. The person who rightly prays hungers and thirsts for God. Most people in the developed world have never really been hungry. At most we have experienced a self-imposed hunger from fasting. I once fasted for 21 days on just water. By the fourth day, I felt really hungry. Every cell in my body was crying out for food. But my situation was somewhat artificial. At any moment I could have grabbed a hamburger or pulled out a "Twinkie." With real hunger comes a sense of desperation—and urgency.

One sees this hunger in the Third World. When I was in Calcutta, India, in 1985, I saw hunger. I saw it in the eyes of an emaciated girl who held out her hands longingly for a piece of bread. I saw it in the face of a dirty, sweating boy who rummaged through the trash in the gutter looking for a discarded sandwich. It is more than being a little hungry or a little thirsty. It is desperation. This is the type of hunger and thirst we must have for God. The heart that finds is the heart desperate for God.

Only God Can Satisfy

In the Bible a hunger for God always ends in prayer. Psalm 143:6 notes, "I spread out my hands to you; my soul thirsts for you like a parched land." The psalmist obviously strongly desired to be close to God. His desire led him to prayer.

> How lovely is your dwelling place,
>   O Lord Almighty!
> My soul yearns, even faints,
>   for the courts of the Lord;
> my heart and my flesh cry out
>   for the living God. (Psalm 84:1-2)

The psalmist longs to enter the court of God and worship at his dwelling place. He feels an absence of God. He cries out to be in God's presence. This feeling of isolation and separation leads the psalmist to urgent prayer: "Hear my prayer, O Lord God Almighty; listen to me, O God of Jacob" (Psalm 84:8).

The reason we urgently go to God in prayer is because we believe that only he can satisfy our spiritual hunger. We have tried to find satisfaction by other means. We have turned to sports, work, pleasure and fame. Yet as the preacher in Ecclesiastes noted, all these pursuits are a "chasing after the wind" (Ecclesiastes 1:14).

God Invites Us to Find Satisfaction in Him

> "Come, all you who are thirsty, come to the waters; and you who have no money, come, buy and eat! Come, buy wine and milk without money and without cost" (Isaiah 55:1).

God freely offers us the most satisfying elixir that we will ever taste. Once we taste his potion, nothing else compares.

> The Lord will guide you always; he will satisfy your needs in a sun-scorched land and will strengthen your frame. You will be like a well-watered garden, like a spring whose waters never fail (Isaiah 58:11).

Are you trying to find satisfaction some other place? What does your schedule or your checkbook say about where your confidence lies—about what you really believe in—about what you really yearn to have? Are you desperate, daring and urgent in your drive to know God more deeply? Would you let anything stop you from seeking him?

We Must Desire God Alone

Many people fail to have satisfying prayer lives because they are double-minded when they pray. James 4:3 describes the one who asks God, but does not receive anything because he asks with the wrong motives that he may spend what he gets on his own pleasure. Prayer is not for those who want God to "rubber stamp" their desires. It is for those whose greatest desire is fellowship with God. Prayer is not for those who do it to get what they want, but for those who do it to get what God wants.

To wholeheartedly pursue God, we must do our best to rid ourselves of all distractions which might keep us from focusing on God. Our prayer times should be holy ("set apart") times—free of any disturbance. Find a place that you can call your own. Let it be away from the phone or the door. Let your family know that prayer time can only be disturbed by an emergency. Unless you passionately fight for time alone with God, it will not happen.

God Blesses the Hungry Heart

When we pray rightly and righteously, it allows God to work powerfully in our lives. Jesus said, "Blessed are those who hunger and thirst for righteousness, for they will be filled" (Matthew 5:6). They will be filled—it will happen. "Ask, and it will be given to you; seek and you will find; knock and the door will be opened to you. For everyone who asks, receives; he who seeks finds; and to him who knocks, the door will be opened" (Matthew 7:7-8). Those who seek will not be denied. James said, "You have not because you ask not" (4:2 KJV). When we passionately seek God, he richly blesses us. This was true of the nation of Judah. 2 Chronicles 15:15 states: "All Judah rejoiced about the oath because they had sworn it wholeheartedly, they sought God eagerly, and he was found by them. So the Lord gave them rest on every side." When they sought God wholeheartedly, he blessed them.

Sometimes we must wrestle in prayer to receive the blessings of God. If we desire a blessing wholeheartedly, then we will be willing to wrestle for it and even wait for it. Jacob, the son of Isaac, wrestled for a blessing with a man sent from God. Genesis 32:26 says, "Then the man said, 'Let me go, for it is daybreak.' But Jacob replied, 'I will not let you go unless you bless me.'" Jacob received his blessing. He received it because he greatly desired it—enough to wrestle for it; God blesses the hungry heart.

The power of your prayers is not dependent on your achievement, your knowledge, your age, your personality or your popularity. It is dependent on the hunger in your heart for the person of God and the will of God. No hungry heart will ever be turned away.

Prayer

Dear Father, as a deer pants for a spring of water, so my soul yearns for you, my God and my Father. I wholeheartedly seek to dwell in your presence every moment of every day. When I stray from you, I feel incomplete, helpless and hopeless in a war-torn world.

Keep any and every distraction away from me. Do not let me lose for one moment your presence in my life. I know that without you I am nothing. If ever I presume to attempt life on my own, awaken me to the folly of my action.

Dear Lord, my soul thirsts for you as a sun-parched land desires water. Come and quench my thirst. Come and satisfy my hunger. Fill me with your Spirit and your truth so I may never be hungry again. In Jesus' name. Amen!

FOR FURTHER STUDY:

Psalm 63
Psalm 73
Psalm 103

7
Full of Faith

Chris McGrath

> When the servant of the man of God got up and went out early the next morning, an army with horses and chariots had surrounded the city. "Oh, my lord, what shall we do?" the servant asked. "Don't be afraid," the prophet answered. "Those who are with us are more than those who are with them." And Elisha prayed, "O LORD, open his eyes so that he may see." Then the LORD opened the servant's eyes, and he looked and saw the hills full of horses and chariots of fire all around Elisha (2 Kings 6:15-17).

Full of Faithlessness

Fear. Discouragement. Alarm. Dismay. Just some of the emotions that must have swept over Elisha's servant as his head rose above the parapet of the city of Dothan and he spied the legions of Aram camped around the walls. We never learn his name, but many of us can relate very closely to this character for one simple reason: at this point in his life, he lacked faith, and we all have known what it is like to lack faith at some point in our Christian lives.

Elisha's servant only saw the chariots and soldiers of Aram and the immediate threat that they posed to his life. When we lack faith, we only see the world around us and the challenges that life is throwing at us. Even though Elisha, the prophet of God, was standing right next to him, he felt fearful and discouraged. When you wallow in faithlessness, your Bible study lacks power and your eyes skim the pages without absorbing the words. Elisha's servant was aware of the problems but oblivious to the saving presence of God. Are you like that?

In January 1987, I left London with my wife, Jaqueline, to lead a mission team to Australia. We led the work there for three years, but in November 1989, we were called back to London so that we could work on our marriage. Those leading us felt that we should stay until January of 1990 before returning once again to Australia. As it turned out, we were unable to secure the kind of visa that we wanted at that time, and so we delayed our return until July. At the time, all that I could see was that I'd lost the leadership of Australia. I began to feel like a nobody in the London church. I developed an attitude of resentment towards God to the point that I lost my trust in him. I had been taken away from my dream of leading the movement of God in Australia and could see nothing good in my life. As a result, I stopped praying and reading my Bible for two weeks. I couldn't see how God could change my situation or how anything positive could come out of it. I was just like Elisha's servant: faithless, discouraged and miserable.

Finding Faith

As he looked down on the Arameans, the servant's mind began to race and he turned in despair to Elisha. He admitted that he needed help, acknowledged what was going on in his heart and the discouragement that he was feeling. Because of his humility, he found the help that he needed.

I got to the point where I knew that something had to be done. I knew that it was wrong to go for two weeks without studying my Bible or praying. I knew that my attitude towards God was wrong. As a result, I spent a day in the park with God, a day that I will never forget. That day I went out to fight with God. I screamed, I cried, I beat the ground and I got gut-wrenchingly honest with God. I told him I didn't like his discipline, that he wasn't fair and how I had taken my whole family to Australia and given up everything to serve him, only to have the carpet pulled from under my feet. I told God that I didn't like him or my relationship with him. As I prayed, I gradually began to realize that God was not the problem and that I was the problem. I ended up apologizing and seeking forgiveness. When I turned to God, I got my relationship with him back again.

When I left the park that day, I decided in my heart that I was going to trust in whatever God had planned for my life and that I would be content with whatever he gave me. When you see the challenge facing you, do you collapse in a heap of self-pity and discouragement, or do you go out and get the help that you need from your brothers and sisters? Do you ask for the help that you need from God? How honest are you in your prayer life? Do you babble like a Pharisee or have you gotten gut-level honest with God about how you are feeling and where you are at? These are the prayers of power that will change your life. (Mark 9:23-24).

Seeing Through Faith

When Elisha's servant got humble and trusted his leader, God opened his eyes and he was able to see through faith what he had been unable to see before. As he looked out again, he was able to see the Aramean soldiers as before, but this time he saw something that filled him with hope, joy and faith. As he looked at the hills, he saw that the Arameans were themselves surrounded by the army of heaven. Everywhere he looked, he saw fiery chariots and horses-suddenly the problem of the Arameans didn't seem quite so daunting. Problems always look less daunting when you get God in the picture and decide to be full of faith.

The day I got right with God, I was sitting and talking with Jackie who is from Milwaukee but has chosen to live her life on the mission field. She asked me if I thought that we would ever go and lead a church in the States. From my faithful, positive, righteous heart, I answered her, "No way." Yet, *that very same day,* I received the call asking if I would be willing to lead the church in Indianapolis, Indiana, *U.S.A.* Within seven days, we were on a plane to Indianapolis. We spent some of the most enjoyable and fruitful months of our Christian lives with the church there. In time, God brought us back to London where we would eventually lead the church and the churches in the United Kingdom. In hindsight, I can now see through eyes of faith what God had in store for me and that God does work for the good of those who love him.

How faithful are you about the challenges facing you today? How optimistic are you? Do you have the eyes of faith that God wants you to have or have you become humanistic and negative? How humble are you in seeking help from God and from your leaders? If you are not doing well in these areas, find the faith that Elisha's servant found: Acknowledge the situation that you're in. Get humble. Decide to trust God. Ask your leaders for help. Ask God for help. Then watch God change your life.

Prayer
This is the prayer that I prayed that day in the park:

God, I know I've needed to do this for a long time. I know that my attitude towards you is not right. I feel cold towards you. I don't feel like I love you anymore, yet I know in my heart of hearts that I do and I want to get this relationship back. I feel like your discipline this time is too hard. You've hurt me and I don't feel like you care. You come across to me as an unloving God. You use us for your own gain. I feel bitter, angry and unhappy, yet I know that what I feel in my heart isn't true. I've allowed Satan to dominate my soul and he has caused havoc between you and me. I've needed to talk to you honestly because I want to get my relationship back with you. I am a brute beast in sin. I know that you are God and that you are forgiving and righteous. Please forgive me for ever allowing these evil thoughts to flood into my mind and destroy my soul. These tears I shed for two reasons: because of the hurt and the pain that I feel and because of the joy I feel from knowing that in trusting you I am doing what is right. I'm sorry. I love you. I will change now. You are my Savior. You are sovereign in my life and I want to glorify you. In Jesus' name, Amen.

FOR FURTHER STUDY:

Judges 6-7
2 Kings 4:32-35
2 Kings 20:1-3

8
Surrendered and Submissive

GORDON FERGUSON
McKenney, Texas

> Going a little farther, he fell to the ground and prayed that if possible the hour might pass from him. "Abba, Father," he said, "everything is possible for you. Take this cup from me. Yet not what I will, but what you will" (Mark 14:35-36).

Talking about the subject of surrender is easy, but actually surrendering everything to God is decidedly difficult. The higher the stakes, the more difficult the process. When Jesus was in the Garden of Gethsemane, he faced the most demanding decision of his life. Yet, he had a heart determined to remain surrendered to the will of God in spite of the cost involved. In one brief account, he shows us what surrender really is and demonstrates exactly how it is accomplished.

Surrender means to put oneself and one's future totally into the hands of God. Notice that Jesus stated very pointedly just what his desires were. But he concluded with surrender: "Yet not what I will, but what you will." Surrender is unconditional and total—*nothing* is held back. Jesus was struggling mightily with facing the cross, but he was determined to obey God in spite of the struggle. True surrender counts the cost of the worst scenario possible and is still willing to pay that price, if paying it is the will of God.

What Jesus Shows Us

What do we learn from Jesus in this most difficult night of surrender? First, we see that he included other people in his prayer struggle—he wanted company at such a time. Some of us are inclined to try working everything out on our own. On the other hand, some are inclined to only talk through challenges with others, and do not struggle in prayer with God the way Jesus did. The former type of person lacks humility and the latter lacks faith. Jesus lacked neither, and his prayer experience shows it. Do you tend toward one of these extremes?

Second, Jesus was totally honest with all of his feelings before God and other men. When is the last time that you told God or another person that you were "overwhelmed with sorrow?" Too many of us have far too little transparency about our lives at the feeling level. Again, pride is the culprit, and we need to deal decisively with this horrible sin. We are far too quick to excuse our pride (in whatever form) with the statement that "Everyone has pride." That only shows the seriousness of the problem. It in no way excuses it! Everyone also lusts. Should we therefore take *that* sin lightly? We need to get all of our emotional struggles out into the light, thereby severely limiting Satan's power in our lives (John 3:19-21).

Third, Jesus did state his preferences to God very clearly. Sometimes we are *too* quick to say "Thy will be done." We cannot make difficult decisions without expressing all of our desires to God (and to others). Once we do talk out all of those desires, then we must make a decision to surrender them. But before preferences can be *crucified,* they must be *stated.* We are designed by God himself to function emotionally in this manner. He knew that spiritual struggles would be the exercise which builds spiritual muscles.

Fourth, our great Example prayed until his surrender was *complete.* He went back to his prayer battle three times. Once he reached the total surrender stage, he found the strength to face the cross and all the events which led to it. In fact, he was the only person to respond calmly in the entire chain of events, because he had claimed the peace which "transcends all understanding." That peace can be claimed only by this process that we are calling *surrender,* which cannot be completed without this kind of prayer (Philippians 4:6-7).

The Testing of Our Surrender

Through the years, God has tested my surrender level many times. Sometimes the testing followed great victories (as was the case after Jesus' own baptism in Matthew 3:13-4:11). Sometimes the testing came along at the very difficult times. God knows exactly *how* and *when* to send these tests in order to help us discover where our hearts really are and where they need to be! Sometimes the tests come in dramatic ways and sometimes they come in ordinary ways, but come they do!

Several years ago, I was challenged to move to Boston for more training and to give up leading the church in San Diego (which I dearly loved—it was my *Philippi*). Later I was challenged to give up leading a church planting to Dallas in order to remain and serve as an elder in Boston. These two dreams of mine had to be crucified, but they did not die easily or quickly. I prayed and wept much before surrendering to those decisions. Looking back, both decisions were *obviously* the best for me and for the kingdom.

About a year ago, a memorable test came in a more ordinary type of life setting. Both my mother and Theresa's mother were coming up for a two-week visit to celebrate Theresa's 50th birthday. At that particular time, I was facing a writing deadline for my longest book to date—*Love One Another*. And as usual, I was already behind schedule. The day they were to arrive, I went out for a prayer walk. Emotionally, I felt very stressed (unsurrendered!) and even thought to myself that writing as much as possible that day might be more important than spending time in prayer (obviously an *unspiritual* thought!). After walking and praying for an hour, I was still quite stressed. As I was fighting the temptation to give up and go back to my writing, I saw an old railroad track going through a deserted area. I immediately turned in that direction and walked down the track praying for surrender. After another hour, I was completely surrendered and at peace with God, myself and my situation. Two weeks later, a very enjoyable visit by our mothers drew to a close and my writing was finished. More importantly, I had been calm and surrendered all during that period of time. Surrender is not simply a nice little theory—it is a wonderful reality when we are determined to imitate our Master's example and claim his faith!

Prayer

Dear Father, as I come to you today, I know that I desperately need to surrender to this situation in my life. With my mind, I know that it is the right thing, but with my heart I am pulled in the other direction. Lord, forgive me for my lack of faith. Help me to surrender my will to your will. I want to do it, God, but it seems so hard right now. Like the man prayed to Jesus, "I do believe, help me overcome my unbelief," I now pray to surrender, but please help me overcome my "unsurrender."

God, I remember the prayer of Jesus in the Garden. Please give me that same heart. Give me the desire to please you at all costs. My heart is so selfish and his was so unselfish.

Lord, I know that the very hairs of my head are numbered, as are the days of my life. Help me to see the sheer stupidity of wanting to hold back from your control. I don't know what is best, and you always know. I need to surrender, and God, I want to surrender, and now I'm going to surrender. Take my life and do with it what you want. Whatever you know is right in this situation, just work it out. You be God, and I'll simply be your servant and your son. Thank you for loving me and for helping me to surrender to your love, even at this moment.

For Further Study:

Luke 9:23-24; 14:25-33
John 12:24-26
1 Corinthians 15:9-10
2 Corinthians 12:7-10

9
Persistent and Determined

THERESA FERGUSON
McKenney, Texas

> Then Jesus told his disciples a parable to show them that they should always pray and not give up..."And will not God bring about justice for his chosen ones, who cry out to him day and night? Will he keep putting them off? I tell you, he will see that they get justice, and quickly. However, when the Son of Man comes, will he find faith on the earth?" (Luke 18:1, 7-8).

Jesus said that we must become like little children if we are to enter the kingdom of heaven (Matthew 18:3). One of the greatest characteristics of little children is that they know how to get what they want. Even as infants, they are determined to gain the attention of their parents and get their needs met. When Bryan and Renee were babies, I remember the many nights that they kept on crying until I awoke from a deep sleep and attended to them. Through their childhood years, they strongly maintained that tendency to be very persistent and determined to obtain what they wanted.

From one viewpoint, such persistence as *adults* may seem self-focused. However, Jesus clearly taught us that in prayer we must be very determined as we cry out to God. At the very foundation of persistent prayer is the faith that a loving God will answer with just what we really need. In our society of "instant satisfaction" and "quick fixes," patience is not a common virtue. But biblical prayer demands both patience and persistence.

A Persistent Woman

One of Jesus' best known teachings on persistence in prayer is found in Luke 18:1-8. The persistent widow kept on seeking justice from an unjust judge until she received it. The Lord said that we needed to learn some vital lessons about prayer from her example.

One lesson is that we must seek *justice,* which means that we seek what is right in the sight of God, rather than what is right in our own sight. God will always answer our prayers. The answer may be "Yes," "No," or "Wait awhile." However, his answers are always based on what is best for us in the situation about which we are praying.

Another lesson in this account is that we must *cry out.* This means that we are urgent, passionate and yet humble. Nice little quiet time chats with God may have their place, but if we are really to move God, it will take some desperate times of pleading and weeping. Remember that during the earthly life of Jesus, "he offered up prayers and petitions with loud cries and tears to the one who could save him from death, and he was heard because of his reverent submission" (Hebrews 5:7).

As young marrieds, Gordon and I learned through some hard times just how important such prayer was. Following a trouble-free pregnancy, we were blessed with the birth of our son Bryan. We had hoped to have a little girl within two years of his birth. However, I had one miscarriage and then another. When I became pregnant for the fourth time, complications arose exactly like those which led to the two miscarriages. Gordon and I were alarmed and somewhat heavy-hearted, but we made the decision to beg God constantly as long as there seemed to be any hope at all. After months of unashamed begging, God blessed us with our daughter, Renee Hope.

Later, as we faced the challenges of leading our children through their teen years, our prayer lives remained just as urgent. God continued to answer us as we maintained our perseverance and determination. We are very thankful today that both of our children are faithful disciples.

In the parable of the widow, Jesus points us to the importance of praying *constantly* (day and night). While it is crucial to begin each day with prayer (Psalm 5:1-3), this should be only the beginning of a day filled with prayer. In 1 Thessalonians 5:17 Paul says to pray continually. This is praying day and night. It also means praying when times are good and when they are bad. (Unfortunately, most of us are far more urgent about praying to have personal needs met than to praise God for needs already met.) Further, it means that we pray for ourselves *and* for others. Actually, if we are to "consider others better than ourselves" (Philippians 2:3), our prayers should reflect that focus. Does that convict you?

Finally—Faith

Finally, Jesus tied this kind of prayer to *faith.* He promised that the right kind of prayers would gain quick justice, but he concluded the parable in Luke 18:1-8 with the question of whether he would find faith on earth when he came. Does the kind of prayer described in this passage reflect the faith in your heart? Do you pray with this kind of persistency and urgency? If not, can you say that you really have faith? A passage like this one should cause many of us to dramatically change the way we pray.

When I think of persistent and determined prayers I think of some special all-night prayer times. Some of these times were to seek changes in my own character, some were for the needs of other disciples, and some were for evangelistic goals. When I put myself so totally into prayer, God always rewarded me richly. He not only changed the situations about which I prayed—he changed *me!* To me, praying with persistence and determination is not simply theory. It is what I have practiced over a period of many years in many different circumstances. It is a precious part of my walk with my Father, and it is the means through which he has so abundantly blessed my life as a disciple, my marriage of 30 years, and my family. *Persistent and determined*—it describes the heart that finds the blessings of God!

Prayer

Dear loving Father, I love you with all of my heart! You are my perfect Parent who always gives me what I need when I need it. I can trust your love and care for me. No one has ever loved me as you have. I come as your child begging to have your heart. Hear the deep desires of my heart to really love the lost and the saved like you do. I know that you want the lost to be saved and your children to be fruitful even more than I do. God, please help me to do everything I can to influence them, and help me to pray with the persistence that activates your great power.

Father, I know that having persistent prayer is based on my faith in you. Help me to overcome everything that would weaken my faith and my prayers. Sometimes my own physical tiredness tempts me to cut short my times with you. Help me to fight the self-focus and to really focus my mind on you and on the needs of others. Lord, I also struggle with perseverance when disappointments come. It really hurts when people are not open to hearing about you, and it especially hurts when they start out being interested and then turn away. Please give me the love for you to feel your disappointment at such times, and help me not to focus on my own disappointment.

Father, help me to deal with the distractions that come along to hinder my prayers, especially when I start focusing on tasks rather than on people. Keep me praying continually when I am out sharing my faith. Help me never to lose heart and give up praying or sharing. I love you with all of my heart. In Jesus' name, AMEN!

FOR FURTHER STUDY:

Psalms 5, 17, 20, 22
Matthew 15:21-29
Luke 22:39-46

10
Eager to Act

DEAN AND KIM FARMER
Hollis, New Hampshire

The king said to me, "What is it you want?"
Then I prayed to the God of heaven, and I answered the king, "If it pleases the king and if your servant has found favor in his sight, let him send me to the city in Judah where my fathers are buried so that I can rebuild it" (Nehemiah 2:4-5).

So we rebuilt the wall till all of it reached half its height, for all the people worked with all their heart.
But when Sanballat, Tobiah, the Arabs, the Ammonites and the men of Ashdod heard that the repairs to Jerusalem's walls had gone ahead and that the gaps were being closed, they were very angry. They all plotted together to come and fight against Jerusalem and stir up trouble against it. But we prayed to our God and posted a guard day and night to meet this threat (Nehemiah 4:6-9).

Jerusalem was in ruins. Years earlier the city had been destroyed and the Jews taken into captivity. While a first wave of Jews were allowed to return to Jerusalem to rebuild God's temple, the city walls still lay in ruins. Upon hearing of the dismal plight of the Jews in Jerusalem, Nehemiah prayed to God (Nehemiah 1:5-11) and asked King Artaxerxes for not only permission to return, but also for financial help in rebuilding the walls. The king granted this request. During the rebuilding, Nehemiah and the Jews encountered fierce opposition. Nehemiah dealt with this obstacle with prayer and an eagerness to act, and by so doing was able to complete the wall of Jerusalem and give the Jews the security of living in a defensible city.

Walking the Talk

Nehemiah turned his theology into biography. He walked his talk. Nehemiah prayed to a powerful God, but it did not end there. Nehemiah was eager and ready to act after his prayer. Many times we, as disciples, pray to God (talk) and then sit back (no walk), waiting for a miraculous solution to appear. This reminds me of a story I heard:

There was once a flood. A man was stranded on the roof of his house. A boat came by to rescue the man. The man replied, "I've prayed to my God—he'll save me!" A helicopter came to save the man, but the man yelled back, "I've prayed to my God—he'll save me!" Finally, the man drowned and went before God. He asked God, "Why didn't you save me from the flood?" and God replied, "I sent you a boat, then a helicopter. Why did you just sit there?" God will provide solutions for every situation, but we must be eager to seek and act upon these solutions (1 Corinthians 10:13).

Nehemiah prayed often and spontaneously (1:4; 4:4, 9; 5:19; 6:9, 14; 13:14, 22, 29, 31). But his prayers were followed by decisions (2:5), plans (4:9, 13, 16) and actions (2:18). God expects us to do his revealed will—saying "Lord, Lord" is not enough (Matthew 7:21). "If anyone turns a deaf ear to the law, even his prayers are detestable" (Proverbs 28:9). What closes God's ears to our prayers is not the depth of our sin, but the lack of our eagerness to act upon his Word. "He who works his land will have abundant food, but he who chases fantasies will have his fill of poverty" (Proverbs 28:19). To pray for personal fruit without evangelism is a fantasy; to pray for repentance without confession is a fantasy; to pray for weight loss without dieting is fantasy. Are you a disciple who "works his field" or merely chases fantasies?

Bringing This Message Home

At the end of March 1993, Kim and I were married. Nine days later, we were leading the church in Berlin, Germany. New marriage, new church, new culture, new language and new relationships—all at once. There were a lot of new responsibilities in my life. I thought I was handling them in a godly, spiritual way.

After a couple of months, I became short with Kim. I would quickly become angry in my heart with her, even about trivial matters. I began to yell at her and say ugly words—words meant to hurt. Afterwards, I felt remorse and asked for forgiveness from God and Kim. Things would change for a while, then my ungodly reactions would be back, but usually worse than the time before. After my outburst of anger, I would be devastated by what I had done. I couldn't believe it. I became desperate. I prayed to change, but I didn't. I hadn't made serious decisions to confess the sin or make a plan to change it and act upon it. I became hopeless. I was afraid of being open. Satan told me, "They won't accept you," "They won't understand," "You can't be an evangelist any longer."

I prayed, but nothing changed. Finally, I saw that I needed to back up my prayers with action. I made a decision to confess all my sin and to get help to make a plan to change, and then to act on that plan. I was encouraged by my wife's reaction—she supported me and stood by me. Tears come to my eyes when I remember the reactions of special friends and leaders like Randy and Kay McKean, Gordon and Theresa Ferguson, Wyndham Shaw and Al Baird. They accepted me and loved me as a son, but they also were urgent and indignant about my need to repent.

First, I prayed to our great and awesome God. Then, I made a decision that frustration is not trusting God, which is practical atheism and therefore sin. I made a specific plan about how to react to different situations and to be open if I failed. I memorized this plan and I was eager to joyfully put it into action. As with the beginning of changing any habit, it was challenging. I received much help from Gordon and Theresa. I prayed every day about my decision, and I looked at my plan daily to remind myself where I was going. In the last seven months, I have not lost my temper, and Kim and I have had maybe five "bumps." All of these have been resolved in less than a few minutes. Our marriage is filled with joy and laughter and purpose. I am now so confident in our marriage that I invite anyone to watch us for one week to see what true Christian marriage is all about. To God be the glory!

What character sin do you pray about every day? Now, what are your specific plans for change in these areas?

Prayer

You are a great and awesome God. Through your Word I see your unconditional love in that Jesus died to give me a chance to have a relationship with you. My desire is to show you my love by eagerly obeying your will.

I come before you with a humble heart, and I want to confess my sin of not loving and sacrificing for the lost like you do. I know, Father, your desire is for everyone to be saved. God, I pray to be urgent in sharing my faith every day. I praise you for the peace, joy and relationships that I now have to share about. Father, I know that saying "Lord, Lord" and not doing your will is hypocrisy, and you hate hypocrites. Place a fire in my heart to sacrifice in helping others become Christians.

I pray, Father, that you help me to be personally fruitful in the next three months. I promise to share my faith everyday with someone new. I promise to be bold in situations where I am normally afraid. I will make no more excuses. Give me the wisdom to organize my schedule so that I can use my free time to study the Bible with my friends.

Father, thank you for showing me your love through my brothers and sisters. Thank you that I can be open with them about my promises to you and that they can help me bring glory to you. Thank you most of all for loving me enough to send Jesus to show me what life is all about. I love you with all my heart, and I am eager to live for you. In the name of Jesus Christ, Amen.

FOR FURTHER STUDY:

1 Chronicles 5:18-22
Esther 4:14-17
Psalm 119:145-146
Proverbs 18:9
Ecclesiastes 10:18

THE
WAY TO
PRAY

*Looking at specific ways we should
pray and some of the ways we can exercise this
powerful spiritual discipline*

11
Praise and Thanksgiving

LEIGH KINNARD
New York City, New York

Be joyful always, pray continually, give thanks in all circumstances, for this is God's will for you in Christ Jesus (1 Thessalonians 5:16-18).

There is power in praise and in thanksgiving. There is power in looking at what God has done and then rejoicing and being grateful. If this were not powerful, God would not call for it. *Pray continually.* But what should be the content of those continual prayers?

This book is full of ideas, but shouldn't praise and thanksgiving be right at the top of the list? Can we possibly have a powerful, life-changing relationship with God if we only bring him more requests—if we don't take the time to praise him and be thankful?

God's will is for us to be grateful—to be joyful always. When we make the decision to be thankful in every circumstance, understanding that God is always working for our good, we are motivated and energized. We want to read the Bible. We want to share our faith. We want to talk even more to God. We want to be discipled. We find it so much easier to be forgiving and encouraging to others. We want to be open. We are excited when someone will listen. In "our joy" (Matthew 13:44) we want to do whatever it takes to fulfill God's will for our lives.

Burdened or Blessed

God's plan is a blessing not a burden (1 John 5:3). But haven't most of us seen how easy it is to get our eyes off our blessings and to focus instead on the challenges and difficulties of life? Gratitude and discipleship should naturally go together—yet sometimes we let discipleship itself burden us. I recently found myself "burdened" by moving and taking over a new ministry when I had every reason to be happy. I felt emotional and negative and, consequently, unproductive. At that time, a sister shared with me how she realized she had become ungrateful in her life. A knife went right through my heart as I realized that I, too, was ungrateful. So I opened up the Word, and the sword started slicing and dicing. My heart developed deep convictions, and I was set free from my selfishness. I had become ungrateful for my life and the family of God. I was so ashamed. Once we lose our gratitude, we have lost everything. We become a walking bad attitude—"full of bitterness and captive to sin." (Acts 8:23).

Growing in Gratitude

How can we keep grateful hearts? What can we do so that praise and thanksgiving will always be in our prayers?

1. *Realize God has chosen us.* "But you are a chosen people, a royal priesthood, a holy nation, a people belonging to God, that you may declare the praises of him who called you out of darkness into his wonderful light"(1 Peter 2:9). God chose you for the purpose of declaring his praises—to tell the world how awesome he is! That is our purpose and absolutely nothing else will fulfill us. Do you really feel humbled because out of all the people on this earth, God picked you? God had the vision that you could actually be like his child! That continually amazes me and motivates me.

2. *See God in everything.* "...joyfully giving thanks to the Father, who has qualified you to share in the inheritance of the saints in the kingdom of light" (Colossians 1:11-12). Train your mind to look at God and not self. Ask yourself "What does God want me to see here?" Learn to see through God's eyes, letting him show you the opportunities and not the obstacles. As you see all the blessings God is placing in your path, you will develop a thankful heart.

3. *Express and verbalize your gratitude.* "Show me, O Lord, my life's end and the number of my days; let me know how fleeting is my life. You have made my days a mere handbreadth; the span of my years is as nothing before you. Each man's life is but a breath"(Psalm

39:4-5). If you found out you only had 14 days left on this earth, what would you do differently? What would you communicate to others? To your spouse? To your children? To people in your life day to day? To someone in your past? Understand that gratitude unexpressed is gratitude suppressed.

Are you expressive with God? Several of us challenged each other to pray 30 minutes a day *only thanking God for specific details in our lives.* We were all convicted at how difficult it was not to sneak in a request in the midst of being grateful! Instead of praying for the things we wished would change in certain people, we thanked God for the strengths he had given them. We took this approach in all the areas we could think of, and it was so freeing. Even as some very challenging times set in, we were able to be joyful.

Understand that God deserves our gratitude, and encourage him with prayers of thanksgiving. Being thankful for what he has done will only bring more of his power into our lives.

Prayer

(With help from Paul's Letter to the Ephesians.) Father, I want so desperately to have a heart that continually praises you and thanks you for every spiritual blessing you've given me in Christ. I know you have chosen me to be holy and blameless in your sight. Thank you for seeing me for what I can become and not for my present failures.

It humbles me to know it was your pleasure and your will to choose me. In return, I desire to make you happy by my life, and I submit my will to yours. Thank you for your grace that you give so freely, so unconditionally. Thank you for forgiving me—for letting your baby boy die in my place. It's hard to understand, but it motivates me not to hurt you by my choices.

I am thankful for your spirit that works so powerfully and will help guarantee my spot in heaven along with my heroes. Thank you for the kingdom—for the amazing privilege of being a part of it. Thank you for all the people in my life who help me be more like your son. It brings me to tears as I think that you gave up your child for me.

Thank you for the amazing honor it is to lead in your kingdom. Help me to live a life worthy of your calling. I pray that all of us will be rooted and established in love, that we may have power with all the saints to grasp how wide and long and high and deep is the love of Christ and to know this love that surpasses knowledge—that we may be filled to the measure of all the fullness of God.

"Now to him who is able to do immeasurably more than all we ask or imagine according to his power that is at work within us—to him be glory in the church and in Christ Jesus throughout all generations forever and ever!" Amen.

FOR FURTHER STUDY:

2 Chronicles 20:20-22
Psalms 35:28, 68:19
Romans 2:4
Colossians 2:6-7
Hebrews 13:15

12
Honesty and Openness

Dave Eastman
Indianapolis, Indiana

How long, O Lord? Will you forget me forever?
   How long will you hide your face from me?
How long must I wrestle with my thoughts
   and every day have sorrow in my heart?
How long will my enemy triumph over me? (Psalm 13:1-2).

How many of us have felt this way at some point? It is likely that David wrote this during the time when Saul was hunting him from place to place, a very intense time in his life. What needs to impress us about this prayer of David is not his great faith, nor his meekness before God nor his peace during trial but rather his heartfelt honesty.

Required for Relationships

Honest communication is the crucial element to any great relationship. The most important thing that a man can do for his wife is to talk openly with her. It is the wise father who works hard to communicate with his teenage daughter. And it is the prudent disciple who makes it his goal to communicate honestly and from the heart to his God. The futility of trying to impress the Lord, either with the eloquence or the length of our prayers, should not need to be stated, yet Jew and Gentile alike in Jesus' day fell into that very trap. Jesus addressed both in the Sermon on the Mount:

"And when you pray, do not be like the hypocrites, they love to pray standing in the synagogues and on the street corners to be seen by men... And when you pray, do not keep on babbling like pagans, for they think they will be heard because of their many words. Do not be like them" (Matthew 6:5, 7).

Consider how ludicrous it is to not be real with God! God is omniscient, all-seeing and all-knowing. He knows what is in our hearts. He knows what we need before we ask him. He knows what we are really seeking when we are out of touch with ourselves! Only honesty with God makes sense!

Seen in the Greats

Let us consider together some of God's great men. Moses was a man who, late in life, had incredible faith. Earlier, he was fairly faithless. We find him at the burning bush, arguing back and forth with God. He questions the wisdom of God's choice to use him; he argues his lack of eloquence; finally, he lays out the real issue—he just doesn't want the responsibility—"Send someone else to do it!" We cannot commend him for his conviction, nor his faith, nor his love of duty. But he is real, he is honest—*he gives God something to work with* (Exodus 4:13).

David's psalms catalogue the entire range of his heart's emotions. In Psalm 13, quoted earlier, he writes, "How long, O Lord? Will you forget me forever?" If David had stopped to consider what he was saying, he could have logically deduced that the Omnipotent God never forgets. But this is not about deduction; it is about honesty. That was the way he felt. At times he climbed the mountains of joy. Just as quickly, he could plumb the depths of despair (Psalm 21:1, 22:1).

But lest we be critical toward these great men of God, let us consider our own lives. How many among us can say we are always up, full of faith and joy, consumed with zeal and vigor for God? We certainly strive for these, but our path is full of challenge.

Working It Out with God

I remember when I was appointed to lead my first Bible discussion group. I was completely overwhelmed, so I went out to my favorite prayer spot and poured out my heart. It was not a pretty sight!

Then came the search for a wife. I thought that I had found the perfect girl. We started dating, and things were advancing. I got the call to go into the ministry. In my mind, I had the wedding all planned. But she broke up with me! I had a time with God then. Where was he when I needed him? Why had he singled me out for loneliness? What was his problem, anyway!? Didn't he realize how much I needed a great wife? From the perspective of 11 wonderful years of marriage to an incredible woman, I can logically work out now that God knew better than me, that his plan for me was better than my own (by far)! But at the time, logic was unimportant; the heart had to speak. I had to work it out with him. And if we are not open before God, we don't work anything out.

Hear again the heart of David: "Why, O Lord, do you stand far off? Why do you hide yourself in times of trouble?" (Psalm 10:1-2). David openly expresses what is on his heart, and for the next 14 verses describes the times of trouble. But then he works it out: "You hear, O Lord, the desire of the afflicted; you encourage them, and you listen to their cry...(v.17).

It is in our openness that we hear our faithlessness and can turn away from it. This is the pattern we see in the lives of Moses, of David, of the sons of Asaph. And I've seen it over and over in my own life. Just recently, during a harvest time in the church, I felt that way. We had worked the soil, studied with the people, prayed the prayers— and then it just seemed like nobody was going to become a Christian. I heard myself saying, "God is opposing the ministry," and, "It just doesn't seem like God is listening." Time for a sanity check. Is the one who promised that he will always be with us no longer with us? Obviously not—but that was on my heart, so I expressed it. Then, with some help from a close friend and brother, I repented of my faithlessness and went on.

God wants a relationship with each one of his ever-increasing family of beloved, adopted children. He wants to know our longings, our aspirations, our problems, our anxieties, our doubts, even our sins. He wants to hear our thanks and praise, but does not refuse our complaints. God doesn't want your money, your sacrifices, your church attendance, your incredible leadership abilities, your acts of selfless service so much as he wants what he loves the most—you! With all of your warts, your problems, your doubts, your complaints—you are his greatest treasure!

Prayer

Our perfect heavenly Father, we praise you today for your nature— you are perfect in every way. Thank you that you hear our cries, that you know our thoughts, that you understand what we need better than we ourselves do. Thank you for the incredible people who stand as examples to us—Moses, David, Peter, Paul. We need these people so that we can see our own failings even as we look to learn from theirs.

I thank you for the way you have put up with me through the 18 years of my spiritual life. I see my faithlessness so clearly at times. It does seem at times that you are far off, but I know and believe that you are with me and in me. All my longings lie open before you—you know all things. Help me, God, to be open and real, to pour out my confession and accept your forgiveness. Help me to voice my complaint but to believe in your promise. Help me to stay transparent before you and one day to come into your glorious presence! Through Jesus—Amen!

FOR FURTHER STUDY:

Numbers 11:11-23
Psalm 33:1-5
Psalm 139:1-24
Psalm 38

13
Reasoning with God

RANDY MCKEAN
Kihei, Hawaii

A Canaanite woman from that vicinity came to him, crying out, "Lord, Son of David, have mercy on me! My daughter is suffering terribly from demon-possession."

. . .He replied, "It is not right to take the children's bread and toss it to their dogs" [puppy dogs].

"Yes, Lord," she said, "but even the dogs [wild dogs] eat the crumbs that fall from their masters' table."

Then Jesus answered, "Woman, you have great faith! Your request is granted" (Matthew 15:21-28).

Reasoning with God in prayer is an expression of great faith and God always rewards faith—especially great faith! This is one of the two times in the New Testament when Jesus commends a person for having "great faith." Certainly the Canaanite woman was persistent but, more than that, she *reasoned* with Jesus. Initially, no one listened to her plea. Then she was told "No" with a short explanation. Eventually she was told "No" again with a further explanation. At this point, she began to reason with Jesus which demonstrated a deep belief concerning his ability to heal her daughter. Jesus did not take offense at this—in fact he was quite impressed! He appreciated her expression of great faith.

We Can Change God's Mind

Remember for a moment the persistent widow of Luke 18:1-8. She went to the judge every day and did what anyone would do with a judge—she reasoned her case before him. Each day she must have come with more reasons why he should grant her request. The implications of this are fantastic. By reasoning with God, we can actually change his mind! We cannot change the eternal purposes of God nor the eternal truths of God, but we can change his mind on how his purposes will be accomplished.

In a small way, it is like a quarterback calling plays in a football game. He has one main purpose or objective—to move the ball forward to score points and, therefore, win the game. Someone may reason with him, and he may change his mind and run different plays or use different players. The thing to remember is that the quarterback never changes his mind about his ultimate purpose—to score points that will win the game. God's ultimate purpose (which is no game!) is that as many as possible might be saved, demonstrating before the entire universe the triumphant powers of love, truth, grace and righteousness.

Abraham was a man who reasoned with God in prayer (Genesis 18:23-33) and so was Moses (Exodus 32:11-14). God had decided to destroy the disobedient Israelites and start a new nation through Moses. Since Moses was a descendant of Abraham, God's promise would have been fulfilled and his eternal purpose would have been unchanged. However, Moses gave specific reasons for not destroying them, and God heard those reasons and changed his mind. The prayer of reason was prayed with great humility, for it was prayed by Moses, the most humble of men living at that hour (Numbers 12:3).

True humility is the key to the prayer of reason—we are not telling God what to do as if we knew better—we are expressing our outlook and giving reasons to back up our thinking. To take the time and put forth the effort of reasoning our heart's desires and dreams demonstrates how deeply we believe God has the power and the love to act on our requests.

Answered Prayers

As a one-year-old disciple (18 years old) while beginning my sophomore year in college, I started praying seriously to God for an awesome Christian wife. More specifically, I prayed to get married at the time I would graduate from college, which was less than three years away. With this prayer I knew I would have to confront my pride and insecurities and start initiating a lot more dates! I reasoned with God about needing to find someone who could work with me in the ministry.

On other days I would reason with God about the wisdom of going into the full-time ministry already married. Most of the time I was simply sharing with my Father God my longings and desires to have a beautiful, spiritual woman who would love me, share my dreams and make life more of a joy. I reasoned that this would help me serve him better and that this would fulfill his promise of not only meeting my needs but also fulfilling the desires of my heart. On June 3, 1977, a few days after my last final exam of my senior year of college, God answered with a "Yes"!

Ten years ago while going through a time when I was not abundantly fruitful, I started reasoning with God. One day I would "remind" him that people were lost, that he wanted them saved and that I wanted them saved. I asked him to please let me bear much fruit! The next day I would share about the people my wife and I were meeting—that they were hurting and that I needed to be an example for my congregation. I kept asking him to let me bear much fruit!

On other days I would share with God that I needed disciples to continue evangelizing the neighborhood and city I was about to leave. My consistent plea was to let me bear much fruit! In the next year, 11 people were baptized into Christ from our Bible Talk and neighborhood. Eight of those people were ones we had initially met and studied with. Humble reasoning with God moves him into action. God answered this prayer with a definite "Yes"!

Four-and-one-half years ago I was confronted with the possibility of a move—from leading the Paris church to leading the Boston church. In prayer, I had many good reasons for staying in Paris—I had already made many sacrifices to get there, the greatest need was on foreign soil, I would lose developed relationships, it would mean another move for the kids, and why change what was working so well? I thought these were awesome reasons, but God answered with a "No."

With the perspective of being able to look back on it, I see that some of my "good" reasons were selfish in orientation. I thank God for always knowing what is best. The greater challenge in ministry has produced greater growth in me and having Boston as a home base has allowed much to be done for the evangelization of Europe. Also, the bond in relationships built in my leadership group has been incredibly refreshing, absolutely needed for my spiritual well-being and invaluable to the completion of the ministry God has given me. I love being where I am and doing what I am doing. God is "reasonable" but he may have the better reasons to answer a prayer with a "No."

My daughter, Summer, is 16 years old and my son, Kent, is 13. There have been countless prayers for our two children since their births: "God, help Summer and Kent to grow up to be strong disciples. Help them to love you with all their hearts for all their lives." And with this prayer to God so many reasons humbly given through the years—that I didn't want them to go through the pain that a life of sin causes, that it would be a sadness too heavy to bear if they were eternally condemned, that, just like God wanted his son to make it back to heaven because of his love for him, I desperately desired my kids to go to heaven because I love them so very much. My daughter was baptized into Christ three years ago and is a strong, determined disciple. My son was just baptized for the forgiveness of his sins a few months ago. I praise God!

Prayer

Father, I pray for the evangelization of the world in the life span of those living in my generation, and I pray for a continued evangelized world through the commitment of the succeeding generation. Father, I pray that my eyes would be able to see it, my ears would be able to hear about it and my hands would be able to significantly help do it. This is the desire of my heart. You have promised to give me my heart's desire if I delight in you—

I do love you so much and delight in my relationship with you and know I am nothing without you.

Father, I also pray for those who would stop your Word from going to all nations. I pray they would repent and come to you. Yet, Father, if they will not repent, I pray you will expose their lives and their true motives. You want your name praised, known and glorified in the universe. Therefore, don't let your enemies and those that love evil even seem to triumph at any moment in time. Destroy those that would harm your cause. Let not those who are just beginning in the faith be led astray through deceit. Only allow the persecutions to strengthen the disciples around the world and to strengthen my convictions about following Jesus.

Father, allow the good our church does to be known, that more and more might be saved. I love you. I need you. Thank you for your incredible forgiveness—I need that so much! Use me and even use me up for your cause.

In Jesus' name, Amen.

FOR FURTHER STUDY
Exodus 32: 1-14
Genesis 18: 16-33
Psalm 13: 1-6
(See Appendix on page 145.)

14
Fasting and Focusing

RICHARD ALAWAYE
New York City, New York

"When you fast, do not look somber as the hypocrites do...But when you fast, put oil on your head...and your Father who sees what is done in secret will reward you" (Matthew 6:16-18).

She glanced at her wristwatch for the third time that morning. It was only 10 o'clock. She was very hungry and felt as though she hadn't eaten in two days. Sarah was fasting for the first time in her life, and the thought of going without food for the next 14 hours seemed impossible. She called her discipler, Anne-Brigitte, on the phone saying, "I'm very hungry so I'm breaking my fast." Anne-Brigitte replied, "That's precisely the point of fasting. You will be hungry. Concentrate and focus on God's power." This was my wife, Sarah, as a young disciple a few years ago.

Fasting is never easy. Depriving our taste buds of our favorite meals and dishes can be challenging, but we must accept that fasting is part of the Christian life and is good for us.

"When You Fast"

It is interesting to note that Jesus said "*when* you fast" and not "*if* you fast." Our Lord assumes that fasting will be a regular part of our lifestyle. In the Old Testament, God commanded the Jews to fast on the Day of Atonement (Leviticus 23:27,29) and fasts were frequently called by leaders when there were special needs (see 1 Kings 21:9 and Jeremiah 36:9 for examples). In the time of Jesus, the Pharisees fasted twice a week (Luke 18:12), and clearly the disciples in the first century church were accustomed to fasting (Acts 13:2, 14:23). With no express command given us in the New Testament,

God has left it to our discretion how often to fast. However, that is no reason to neglect this vital spiritual discipline.

Getting Practical

1. *Make it a part of your lifestyle.* We shouldn't wait for trying times before turning to God. Some have stopped fasting as they've grown older as disciples. We should never fall into the trap of being too familiar with God so that we take him for granted. The truth is many of us aren't fasting enough and some, sadly, aren't fasting at all.

2. *Fast with a purpose in mind.* There must be a focus to your fasting: to bear fruit, to find a job, to experience a closer walk with God, etc.

3. *Decide what kind of fast you intend to have:* total abstinence from food and drinks, a juices-only fast, water-only fast, etc.

4. *Decide how long you intend to fast and stick to it:* 24 hours, from sunrise to sunset, three days, seven days, etc. It is quite easy to begin something, but character is needed to see it through.

5. *Seek input from other disciples.* Although Jesus set an awesome example by fasting for 40 days, don't embark on a long fast yourself without seeking advice. The effects of a 40-day "water only" fast can be devastating to the body—even resulting in death. I do know of one leader who did a 40-day "juices-only" fast while another went on a 21-day "water-only" fast. We can follow their sacrificial examples as we make fasting decisions in our lives.

Fasting and Your Future

It is important that we fast before making major decisions in our lives. We should commit things to God through prayer and fasting so that our plans will succeed (Proverbs 16:3). I believe that our destinies will be very different if we will submit ourselves totally to God through prayer and fasting before making critical decisions in our lives.

As I prepared to graduate from law school several years ago, I decided to fast and pray and ask God to reveal where he wanted me to live. I made a vow that I wouldn't break the fast until God made things absolutely clear. Through praying and seeking advice, I concluded by the seventh day of my fast that God wanted me to move to Boston. I spent exactly 10 months in Boston and was asked to be on the mission team going to Nairobi, Kenya. I have been back in Africa for the last five-and-a-half years, and it is amazing to see how God is gradually transforming "the Dark Continent" into the continent of light. How differently would things have turned out had I not fasted and prayed about my decision?

Your Father Will Reward You

Jesus tells us in Matthew that God will reward our sacrifice when we fast. Ezra proclaimed a fast and asked God for a safe journey as the Israelites prepared to return from exile (Ezra 8:21-22). God answered their prayers and protected them from bandits along the way (Ezra 8:31). Just as God protected Ezra, God will answer us as well.

Since our purpose as disciples is to glorify God by bearing much fruit (John 15:8), there could be no greater use of fasting than to find power to help others know God. A brother named Oscar had not been personally fruitful in a long time. He fasted and prayed to meet a guy named "Jeff" who would become a Christian. Several weeks later, he met a man named Jeff; Jeff started coming to church, studied the Bible, and was baptized a short while later!

Recently in Nairobi, three unemployed brothers decided to pray and fast to secure gainful employment. Julius, Thomas and Fred fasted two days each. On the sixth day of their fasting chain, all three brothers got jobs with three different companies. This was no accident. God heard their pleas and rewarded their faith.

As we strive to see this world evangelized in our generation, all of us as disciples must constantly pray and fast so that God will accomplish his purposes through us. Years ago, when Jim Brown was still in Nairobi, he devoted himself to prayer and fasting. God rewarded his group of about 25 disciples incredibly with 12 baptisms in just one month. Recently in Lagos, the church set a goal to have

70 baptisms in one month. A fasting chain went on for the month and God blessed them with 75 baptisms.

God wants to bless and reward us in so many great ways, but we must be men and women who constantly humble ourselves before him and depend on him for everything.

Prayer

Good morning, Father. Holy God, I praise you for being a mighty God. Father, you alone deserve to be praised and worshipped. You are the God who spoke this universe into existence and calls things that are not as though they were. Father, you are my light and my salvation, for I have no other god besides you. Lord, you neither sleep nor slumber and you never get tired of listening to me.

Father, I recognize that I am a sinner and do not deserve to come before your throne. Lord, please forgive me for the times I have fallen short of your grace.

Holy God, I beg that my fasting be acceptable in your sight. I have no one else to turn to at this hour, and I desire to be close to you. Lord, look down with favor upon me as I fast and pray to you. Father, I desire to be personally fruitful. I beg that your Spirit will lead me to someone who desires a relationship with you. Lord, please answer me quickly. Father, give me the strength that I need during this time. Sustain me and walk with me, Heavenly Father. Draw me closer to you. Help me to be totally focused on you, Holy God.

Father, you promise to reward those who fast and pray to you. Lord, hear my prayer and grant me the desires of my heart. I ask this in the precious, holy and mighty name of your Son, Jesus. Amen.

FOR FURTHER STUDY:

Isaiah 58
Luke 2:36-37
Acts 13:1-3

15
Alone and in Private

LARRY AND KIM STRONDAK

As the deer pants for streams of water,
so my soul pants for you, O God.
My soul thirsts for God, for the living God.
When can I go and meet with God?
(Psalm 42:1-2)

Memories of an early morning prayer walk at Loon Mountain remind me (Kim) of the power of private prayer. At 5:00 a.m. I gazed up at the stars and the moon in the cool out-of-doors. The mountains engulfed me in their majesty as I sat perched on a large boulder, waiting to pray with a sister. But she didn't show. God knew that I needed time alone with him.

As I lifted my eyes to the heavens, I started singing hymns to God—one led to another as my heart longed for him to hear my praises and to smile. As I sang, I meditated on God; his grandeur, displayed by the mountains; his beauty, displayed by the stars and moon; his faithfulness, displayed by the daily rising of the sun; and his love, shown by giving us nature to enjoy. Truly men are without excuse in seeing God.

As I continued to pray, I began to cry, thankful to be here but telling God it had been too long since I'd gotten up very early to get out and rejoice in him. Confessing my sins to God, I asked him to forgive me and cleanse my heart, thankful that Jesus' blood would continue to purify me.

What a time I had with God! What a memory God made with me that morning! That day God reminded me of the reasons why we need to pray alone and in private. It is a time we can be completely vulnerable and open with him; to come in touch with how we really feel. It is a time when we can sing his praises, dance around, cry, laugh, confess our sins, or blow God kisses and be in love with him and not feel inhibited because someone else is watching.

Having personal, focused time with God is integral to our spiritual health and growth. The following suggestions can help us to develop powerful prayer lives:

Find a Solitary Place

Mark 1:35, Matthew 14:13, and Luke 4:42 show us that Jesus often went to solitary places to pray. In an age of telephones, beepers, cellular systems, televisions and electronic gadgets, it can be extremely difficult to find a quiet place to pray. Solitude, however, is essential in developing a deep relationship with God. God tells us, "Be still and know that I am God" (Psalm 46:10). Do you have a special place where you can go and meet with God? If not, make one (or several). Not only can you find solitude while walking on a country road, in the mountains, or in your own backyard, but in some unexpected places such as in your own room early in the morning, in your basement, on a rooftop, or in the private pages of your prayer journal. Remember, the beauty of the place isn't as important as the beauty of the relationship.

Get Heart-to-Heart with God

Psalms 5, 38, and 42 are just a few examples of how open and expressive David was with God. David shares everything with God—from joy and delight to anguish and despair. How open are you with God? Do you keep your feelings stuffed deep inside; do you dump them all out on your spouse or roommate; or do you pour them out in prayer to God?

God wants our hearts! As we have both learned to be open and expressive with God, we have been changed. It has deepened the loving feelings we have for God; it has helped us to get in touch with what is really in our hearts. As a result, we are much more open and real with others.

Get Energized!

We can get fired up by sermons, the fellowship and music, but when Jesus needed strength, he went to be alone with his Father. Imagine you've just spent the last day, and well into the night, preaching and teaching and healing. What would you most look forward to? Sleeping in the next day? Not Jesus! What energized Jesus was time with his Father, even at the expense of sleep. During the most draining, stressful and physically grueling times, Jesus sought private time with God (Matthew 11:28).

Expect to Be Changed!

There is nothing in your life that God cannot change. No sin is too big, no character flaw too entrenched, and no ministry too weak that God can't change it. The question is, are you willing to pray about it? Are you willing to wrestle with God, like Jacob, until he changes you or your ministry? (Genesis 32:22-32).

Two years ago, I (Kim) came before our sector and confessed that I had not been personally fruitful in the last seven years as a Christian. I had met two men who later became Christians, and I had studied with many women who had become Christians, but I had never converted a woman whom I had met personally. I decided to be open with it and to wrestle with God until he changed this situation. I decided to pray three times a day for the people I was personally working with, and I fasted for 21 days for God to use me to help save souls.

I prayed for my friend Blair for a whole year, three times a day, wrestling with God for her because she was an atheist. Since that time not only has she become a Christian, but her husband, Tom, has also—along with two other women I met over the last two years. Grab ahold of God; wrestle with him for as long as it takes, and expect to get up and walk away changed.

Make Memories with God!

Use your prayer times to make special memories with God. Great memories of spiritual and fun times in the kingdom help you stay faithful when the hard times come. So it is with your relationship with God. Joshua 4:7 tells of the Israelites setting up stones of remembrance to remind them of what God had done in delivering them from Egypt. In the same way, we can make great memories with God to cherish in our hearts. Here are some ideas: have a special date with God; write him a love letter; sing him a song you composed; write on a balloon and let it go; hang a poster on a wall in your room and write all of the things you love about God on it. The ideas are endless. Do you have many fond memories of the times you've spent together?

Give your heart to God in special prayer times. Don't be too quick to go and to do. Be quick to stay and to pray.

Prayer

Prayer from Kim's mountain time with God:

God, thank you so much. I feel and see how much you always love me. Through times like this, through your Word, and through the disciples in your incredible kingdom, your love shines through. But somehow I want you to feel that love back from ME, God! I want my actions to show love, but I also want my heart to be inside of your heart. I want you to FEEL my passion for you! My heart is full with love for you, God! Can you feel it? As I look up to your stars and smile and blow you a kiss, I like to think that you are sending a kiss back to me.

FOR FURTHER STUDY:

1 Samuel 12:23
Luke 11:1-4
Philippians 4:4-9

16
With Others and in Unity

FRED AND EMMA SCOTT

"Again, I tell you that if two of you on earth agree about anything you ask for, it will be done for you by my Father in heaven. For where two or three come together in my name, there am I with them" (Matthew 18:19-20).

Great spiritual power is available to those disciples who understand unity in prayer and practice it. Before reading this article, ask yourself the following questions:

1. How often this week have I prayed *with* someone?
2. In a troubled time is my first instinct to ask others to pray with me about a problem?
3. Do I pray with others about crucial decisions?
4. Is praying together with others my custom?

If our most common answer is "No," then we are denying one of the most powerful aspects of prayer.

In Acts 1:14 we see that the apostles, along with the women and Jesus' mother and brothers, obviously felt a deep need to pray together in unity. It was their first instinct after the ascension of Jesus for many reasons. With all the mixed emotions of initial grief at the crucifixion, despair and desolation after the burial, incredulity at the reported resurrection and sheer exultation at actually seeing and hearing their risen Lord, these early disciples needed constant prayer to make sense of their situation. Surely this fact alone stands as a challenge to us in the basically self-reliant 20th century. Many of us neglect the power of united prayer because we don't see its importance or truly feel the need. Let's study the book of Acts and see the "Acts 1:14" principle in effect.

Decisions of Destiny

In the aftermath of Judas' suicide, the apostles needed to select his replacement. Two eminently qualified individuals were proposed (Acts 1:15-26). How often have our choices been based on "feelings," "insight" or "wisdom"—apart from prayer? The disciples sought God's guidance through united prayer (verse 24) and the lot fell to Matthias. It was characteristic of the early church to make and seal important decisions with prayer (see also Acts 6:6; 13:3; 14:23).

"Usually" United

One of the most striking aspects of the early church was its devotion to prayer. We see this reliance clearly by watching the lives of the leaders (Acts 2:42). Praying together was nothing unusual, but rather, customary. In Acts 3:1 Peter and John were on their way to pray. Acts 6:4 outlines the apostles' priority. They grouped together for prayer often (Acts 16:13; 16:16). The prerequisite for this action must have been an absolute unity of purpose and dependence on God (Acts 4:32). We have found personally that praying with others is bonding, unifying and brings an extra sincerity and openness to our prayers.

Crisis Calls

Every one of us has been or will be tested in our faith. A crisis will often show us the depth of our faith. During the first major wave of persecution in the first-century church, the disciples raised their voices together in prayer to God (Acts 4:24). They knew that their need was for boldness, not analysis. Imagine the encouragement any of the disciples present would have felt as they left the room speaking the Word of God boldly. The church earnestly prayed for Peter, who was eventually released after angelic intervention (Acts 12:5). In response to united prayer, God will often do the seemingly impossible at the time of human crisis.

When Fred's father, Charles, was diagnosed with terminal cancer, it was one of the most challenging times for our faith. We had been Christians for eight years at the time, and neither of our families had shown the slightest openness. Even after some attempts to discuss spiritual matters, Charles seemed distracted and uninterested in his spiritual condition. After trying every argument and much persuasion, we knew the only answer was united prayer. We decided to spend an hour in prayer together, first thing every morning, imploring God to move Dad's heart.

These times of prayer were some of the most powerful, emotional and vulnerable times of our lives, and drew us closer together as only a crisis can. Miraculously, Dad's heart changed completely and dramatically one evening about a month later. He had started to read the Bible on his own, develop a fear of God and acknowledge his need for salvation. We subsequently studied the Scriptures with him. He was baptized and passed away three weeks later to join his Lord.

Sign of Strength

When we read about the apostle Paul, we marvel at his personal power, limitless strength and fearless conviction. We long to be like this in our own Christian lives. We cannot, however, merely be content with imitating his style. We must also imitate his heart. Though strong and courageous, Paul was clearly dependent on God's strengthening through prayer, particularly in unity with others. After his address to the Ephesian elders, Paul knelt with them in prayer (Acts 20:36-38). Another farewell, this time in Tyre, found Paul kneeling in prayer. We can but speculate on the content of these prayers, but we are sure their sentiment is expressed in Romans 15:30-33:

> I urge you brothers, by our Lord Jesus Christ and by the love of the Spirit, to join me in my struggle by praying to God for me. Pray that I may be rescued from the unbelievers in Judea and that my service in Jerusalem may be acceptable to the saints there, so that by God's will I may come to you with joy and together with you be refreshed. The God of peace be with you all. Amen.

With our great goal of world evangelization we must surely apply ourselves as never before to praying together in unity. God loves for his people to "raise their voices together in prayer!" (Acts 4:24). And he loves to answer the prayers they pray.

Prayer

Dear Father, we know that since the creation of the world, you have always had a plan to be unified with man. Lord, we know that through prayer we can not only be unified with you through the Spirit, but also with our brothers and sisters. Only through unity can this world be won for you, and prayer is the power of unity.

Father, we see through your Word so many great examples of prayer and unity. We think of Jehoshaphat when he faced such a vast army with no idea what to do, but he called upon your mercy and power. He called all the peoples of the town together, and they cried out to you in unity for the victory over Satan's schemes to destroy your people. We saw such a powerful defeat of Satan as they had victory through prayer, singing and rejoicing as they surrendered to you.

We know this leads to an understanding and conviction that the battles we face are yours. We ask that in the same way, with the vast armies we face, that you would give us the victory! Please unify us in mind, thought and purpose. Help us to be unified as we pray for the growth of the kingdom, for the faith of the leadership and the evangelization of the world in this generation. In all these things give us unity in prayer. In Jesus' name. Amen.

FOR FURTHER STUDY:

2 Chronicles: 20:2-20
Nehemiah 9
James 5:13-18

17
In Marriage and Family

BRUCE WILLIAMS
Orange, *California*

Unless the Lord builds the house,
    its builders labor in vain.
Unless the Lord watches over the city,
    the watchmen stand guard in vain.
In vain you rise early and stay up late,
    toiling for food to eat—
for he grants sleep to those he loves.
            (Psalm 127:1-2)

This psalm was written by Solomon, a son of King David. Solomon probably knew the truth of this passage as much as anyone else. He had seen incredible tragedy in his own family which was a direct result of his father's unspiritual leadership. Even though David had begun as a powerful man after God's own heart, he failed to stay close to God and lead his family spiritually. Consequently, his marriages and family were destroyed by lust, jealousy, envy, criticalness, selfish ambition, ingratitude, rebellion and murder. His family stands as a warning to all married disciples of how Satan can destroy the most precious of all human relationships.

The family relationships can be the most rewarding but also the most challenging. We need God! Prayer must be the foundation, the walls and the roof of our family. Let us consider practical ways in which prayer can allow God to be the builder of our house.

The Foundation of a Marriage

Robyn and I have been married for 22 years. During that time, we have prayed together every night before going to sleep. I remember our very first prayer together as husband and wife on our honeymoon night. We pledged our love for one another and prayed to God that our marriage would bring glory and honor to him by impacting many lives for Christ. Now 22 years later, we are closer than ever and have seen God impact incredible numbers of people through us. Our communication, openness, teamwork and sexual relationship are better than we could have ever imagined!

There are powerful benefits of daily prayer with one another:

1. *Prayer keeps your relationship spiritually focused.* Bills, diapers, sickness and routine activities can drown out the fact we are not just husband and wife, but brother and sister in Christ.

2. *Prayer keeps us going to bed united.* Ephesians 4:26-27 teaches that we must not let a day close with unresolved anger. It is impossible for me to pray with Robyn if there are any resentful attitudes within me towards her. Because of my commitment to nightly prayer, this has compelled me to resolve differences.

3. *Prayer makes us more grateful.* We thank God for the day's events and reflect on the blessings.

4. *Prayer gives focus and direction.* Praying about tomorrow keeps us in tune with what is ahead and makes us more united.

Make the decision today that you will pray together every day, from this point on, so long as you both shall live.

Building from Birth

Prayer cannot be just something we do mechanically at meals or bedtimes with our children. Our dependency on God must penetrate every area of family life. Here are some ways to make it happen:

1. *Nightly prayer with children from infancy.* If your children, even as babies, grow up hearing you pray, they will be more motivated to have a personal relationship with God and will have a great example to follow.

2. *Daily devotionals with younger school children.* In order for our children to be spiritually focused for the day and with each other, we had 15-minute morning devotionals before the children left for school. This was the last thing they did before leaving the house. We

usually had a weekly theme that was threaded through every morning time. Scripture memory and practical assignments were incorporated and then we would pray about the day. Once the children became teens, we transitioned into a weekly family devotional on Monday nights.

3. *Taking prayer walks.* Robyn and I both have taken prayer walks with our teenage children. Jason and I just recently took one on the morning of his second spiritual birthday. These walks with God are memorable events in our relationship. Because Brooke and Jason are now both disciples, it is such a joy to hear how much they depend on God.

4. *Quiet times with one another.* There was a time when Brooke and Jason were not very close. They decided to have some quiet times with each other, and this has bonded them like nothing else.

5. *Praying as a family about major decisions and challenges.* There is nothing like going to God and knowing he will provide answers and solutions for whatever happens. This has helped our family to stay spiritually dependent. Praying with children after they are disciplined adds powerfully to the impact of such training.

Having a spiritual marriage and family does not just happen. It requires a deliberate effort to keep God as the builder of the foundation, walls and roof. We can then be confident that God will give us a marriage and family that will be a light to the world and the salt of the earth.

Prayer
(The kind of prayer we have prayed through the years)

Dear God, help us to pray together every day as husband and wife. We know how challenging it can be to have a united and loving marriage. We commit, God, that we will never go to bed angry. We will close the day with gratitude for what you have done and trust that you will work in our lives tomorrow.

Thank you for our children. Help us to lead them spiritually. Help us to be deeply spiritual and not religious. Help us to be an inspiration for our children to love you and commit themselves to you. We look forward to the day when they will be baptized into Christ and begin a new life. In the meantime, help us to teach them how to daily repent and deal with their sinful attitudes. Help us to be an example of how to do that. We commit ourselves and family to you! In Jesus' name, Amen.

FOR FURTHER STUDY:

Malachi 4:6
Luke 1:17
Ephesians 6:4,18
1 Peter 3:7

THE NEEDS WE BRING

The kinds of things God wants for us to bring before his throne and how to wrestle in prayer until we find victory

18
Sin and Transgression

"Forgive us our sins,
for we also forgive everyone who sins against us" (Luke 11:4).

God is God, and we are not. Every time we pray, we come before
a sovereign, omnipotent, omnipresent being who never has and
never will sin. What a challenge! What business do we have communicating with the Maker of the universe? What do we have to offer?
Advice? Conversation? We come to the Creator with nothing more
than impurity—even the very best of us! And that every time we pray!
We are totally at his mercy! We must come to understand that
Jehovah-God has established his *forbiddens*, and yet like a father,
gives his *forgiveness*.

God's "Forbiddens"

Even as early as the Garden, our wise Father made it clear that
life has its forbidden things. In Genesis 2:16-17 he said, "You are free
to eat from any tree in the garden; but you must not eat from the tree
of the knowledge of good and evil..." Yes, he made very clear what
was forbidden.

There is an old tale about a peasant who, while hoeing in his
field during the spring thaw, came across a deadly snake. He raised
his hoe to kill it, but the snake begged for mercy. "I am too frozen to
do you any harm. Please spare my life!" he cried. The farmer, full of
compassion, picked up the half-dead serpent and put it into his tunic
against his chest. As he began to work, the snake got warmer and
warmer. Suddenly, the snake bit the peasant. The peasant frantically
reached into his tunic, pulled out the snake and threw it to the

85

ground. "Why?" asked the dying man of the deceiving serpent. "I befriended you. I trusted you." "True!" hissed the snake as it slithered away, "but do not blame me. You knew I was a snake when you picked me up."

We know well what sin is. Selfishness. Insensitivity. Pride. Impurity. Impatience. Arrogance. Hypocrisy. Laziness. God says "no" to such things. We say "They are harmless." But the Creator's command is our protection. *God forbids to protect.* This truth is essential to those who would pray. Wanting to save us the pain of learning for ourselves what damage sin can do (our unrighteousness tortured his son!), the Father gives us the possibility of a pure life.

But we choose to transgress his infinitely perfect plan. Then when we come to God and try to pray, we feel guilty and distant; we may even blame him for the fall. Perhaps we try to shift the guilt on to the situation or even to the "snake."

However, we must carry the responsibility for our transgressions. Recently my wife Janet said in a concerned and loving way something to the effect of, "Why is it so easy for you to verbally acknowledge your sin and just move on? Why is it so difficult to express your feelings of brokenness?" She was asking the right questions! I am not an "accused" but rather a "deceived" type of person. Brokenness does not come easily! Perhaps you can relate. We must understand that sin hurts God deeply (Jeremiah 8:20-9:3) and that we are personally, 100% responsible for what we have or have not done!

Leaders take warning: Most likely you are prone to an ugly kind of sin. Does your attitude reflect that of the one who said, "God, have mercy on me, a sinner," or that of the Pharisee who loudly proclaimed his purity? (Luke 18:11-13). How do you approach God? Full of self, or in humility?

Humility begins with the truth. We have sinned and God has not. Humble yourself before him. Trust his plan. He has given us his "forbiddens" and we have not paid attention.

God's "Forgiveness"

In his infinite wisdom, the All-Merciful found a way to forgive the unforgivable. *For-give-ness* is an undeserved gift! Jesus taught us to pray, "Forgive us our sins, for we also forgive everyone who sins against us" (Luke 11:4). Although we have no right to demand forgiveness, Jesus says we should pray with expectation.

A son lies to his father. In tears he humbles himself and pleads for pardon. Although deeply disappointed and painfully hurt by his son's sin, the father forgives. When we have this amazing ability as earthly parents, is it not clear to us that our heavenly Father is also ready to forgive and, incredibly, to forget?

God is willing to eradicate our sin! Disciples must understand this! Every week we hear powerful preaching, have challenging discipleship sessions and are encouraged to repent. But we must never forget, "How great is the love the Father has lavished on us, that we should be called children of God! And that is what we are!" (1 John 3:1).

Not long ago, a prominent German newsweekly published accusations against our church, one being that we supposedly abuse our children! My eleven-year-old son Ben took it upon himself to defend his father. Writing the editor, he refuted the accusations by describing what he has personally experienced: love, patience and forgiveness.

This doesn't mean that I have been a perfect dad! It does demonstrate that Ben has forgiven me my failures as a father. Moreover, my daily forgiveness of him has nurtured our friendship; today, we are the best of friends!

God wants to become your best friend. He will stick up for you to the bitter end; indeed, he already has! It is his nature to pardon the penitent—it's his way of saying, "I believe in you!" Jesus said it perfectly to the adulteress in John 8:11, "Then neither do I condemn you; go now and leave your life of sin."

God is God, and we are not! His *forbiddens* teach us respect for him and the power of the dark side. His *forgiveness* teaches us to cherish the friendship he has built. Out of thankfulness we gain the desire to turn ourselves and others from sin (Psalm 51:12-13). Let us go to our forgiving Father in powerful prayer and win the victory over sin and transgression!

Prayer

Father in heaven, I praise you for this opportunity to pour out my heart before you! You know my heart, you see my sin. I praise you that I can, nonetheless, approach your throne with confidence! I praise you for your protection. You are so wise! You know what I need. My sin is ugly before you. As I search my heart, I recognize and confess the sins of_____.

Father, I pray as David did, "Create in me a pure heart, O God, and renew a steadfast spirit within me" (Psalm 51:10). I know that I do not deserve your forgiveness. My sin hurts your heart. You sacrificed your son for my sin. Thank you, Father, for forgiveness. Your grace is what sustains me. Your sacrificial love gives me new hope!

I am so thankful for hope, for a new beginning! Just as you've given me a new start in my conversion, every day you make me fresh and new. God, I rejoice in the knowledge of your forgiveness. I rejoice that your love covers a multitude of sins!

Teach me again how dangerous the dark side is! Teach me never to play with sin. Teach me to search my heart daily and to recognize the symptoms of sin.

Father, you are an awesome and powerful God! You alone deserve the praise and honor of my lips! Give me victory over my sin! In Jesus' name I pray, Amen!

FOR FURTHER STUDY:

Nehemiah 1:4-7
Psalm 32
Psalm 38
Psalm 40:1-3

19
Our Daily Bread

TERRY ADAME
San Diego, California

"Give us today our daily bread" (Matthew 6:11).

"And why do you worry about clothes? See how the lilies of the field grow. They do not labor or spin. Yet I tell you that not even Solomon in all his splendor was dressed like one of these. If that is how God clothes the grass of the field, which is here today and tomorrow is thrown into the fire, will he not much more clothe you, O you of little faith? So do not worry, saying, 'What shall we eat?' or 'What shall we drink?' or 'What shall we wear?' For the pagans run after all these things, and your heavenly Father knows that you need them. But seek first his kingdom and his righteousness, and all these things will be given to you as well. Therefore do not worry about tomorrow, for tomorrow will worry about itself. Each day has enough trouble of its own" (Matthew 6:28-34).

Every one of us has daily needs—needs that so easily can become worries and anxieties if we are not trusting and relying on God through prayer. First, Jesus teaches us to pray, "Give us today our daily bread." Then he calls us to trust that God will meet all these needs.

Matthew 6 came to mean a great deal to me when we were blessed by God to live in India for six years. Daily life was a challenge: learning to eat the spicy food, having water only certain times during the day, finding a good pediatrician for my three small children, health risks, bugs, rats and the daily challenge of being an American who did not speak the local language. There were times I gave in to frustration and a lack of faith, but I grew through my daily reliance on God through prayer. I was able to be totally happy and fulfilled with my life and the daily challenges we faced.

Meeting the Challenge of Worry

While many of us have little concern about having food, shelter and clothing, we have plenty of needs we can worry about—from meeting a deadline to finding a job to paying off the credit card to the growth and development of our children. Dealing with these daily challenges can be the greatest drain on our joy if we aren't responding with prayer and faith. Satan schemes to blind us to God's concern for our daily lives and needs, and before we realize it, we are anxious and have lost our joy because we have not "presented our requests to God" (Philippians 4:6). Satan has us by the throat when we are anxious about our lives.

Webster's Dictionary defines worry as: 1) to torment oneself with or suffer from disturbing thoughts; 2) to fret; 3) uneasiness or anxiety.

We must ask the question: What daily worries plague me? How about thoughts like: *Do I have true friendships? Am I pleasing God? Are my children happy? Will I get married? Am I a good husband, wife, mother or father? Will I succeed in my career or education? Is my health on the decline? Am I meeting the needs of those around me? Can I meet the expectations of my leaders?*

If the enemy can get us to "fret" and be preoccupied with "disturbing thoughts," he knows he will have succeeded in distracting us from our purpose and destroying our effectiveness as disciples. The solution is an open and honest relationship with God. The answer is prayer offered to him who is totally in control and who works for our good in everything that happens. Isaiah describes for us the awesome power of our Father in heaven and his eagerness to use that power to help us:

Do you not know?
    Have you not heard?
The LORD is the everlasting God,
    the Creator of the ends of the earth.
He will not grow tired or weary,
    and his understanding no one can fathom.

He gives strength to the weary
   and increases the power of the weak.
Even youths grow tired and weary,
   and young men stumble and fall;
but those who hope in the LORD
   will renew their strength.
They will soar on wings like eagles;
   they will run and not grow weary,
they will walk and not be faint (Isaiah 40:28-31).

Our Father is the God of the universe. Nothing is too great for him. He knows our needs and has told us to bring them all to him. What more can we ask?

Preparing Us for the Big Ones

Taking our daily needs to God and learning to trust him day by day prepares us for the big challenges that sooner or later will come to all of us. I firmly believe that the daily trials our family faced during our time in India increased my faith and prepared me for greater challenges. One of those came in January 1991.

We were traveling from Boston to India with our three-week-old twins. During a stopover in London, one of them was diagnosed with a respiratory disease called bronchilitis and a secondary infection of pneumonia. As we prayed that God would change the 50:50 odds that he would live, I remember the pain, the hurt and the temptation to mistrust. But through the whole situation, I knew that God was in control and great comfort came from that knowledge and through our prayers. Many others in London, Boston and India also prayed for our son. He made a miraculous recovery and is now a healthy four-year-old!

I am so grateful for the opportunity to have a relationship with the Creator of the universe and to know that he longs to hear me and to meet all of my needs. We must always remember that he is the one who knows what is best and saves us from worrying about tomorrow, which already has enough trouble of its own.

Prayer

Dear Father, I am so grateful to be your daughter. It excites me to look out at the rain and snow to see your power at work. Thank you for being a God who is in control of the weather and all that happens, and yet is the kind of Father and God who knows the very number of hairs on my head. That has always been something that has blown my mind—how you are so different from earthly fathers in that you are so powerful, yet so gentle and in tune with all of my needs.

God, I am so sorry for the times I don't rely on you, when I am anxious and worried. I hurt you and others around me. Please give me more faith and power to overcome my weaknesses and sin. Help me to be continually on the edge and never grow comfortable or become ungrateful for all the blessings and great things you have given me.

Thank you so much for always loving me in spite of my weaknesses. Thank you for all the great blessings you give me and the way you take care of all my daily needs. As I look around at the world, I become more and more aware of the task ahead of me—to reach out and share your Word and the great ways you have changed my life. I cannot even imagine my life without you. I would always be wondering and worrying about my relationships. I am happy and secure in your love for me.

Father, I love you with all my heart. I pray in Jesus' name. Love, Terry.

For Further Study:

Matthew 7:7-11
Matthew 21:18-22
John 14:13-14
1 John 5:14-15

20
Changes in Character

JEANIE SHAW
Glastonbury, Connecticut

Surely you desire truth in the inner parts;
  you teach me wisdom in the inmost place (Psalm 51:6).

As I write this article I look at a piece of torn, battered paper that is like an old friend to me. It is a page from my prayer list that is prayed through over and over again. I purposely did not type it up to look fancy, because I wanted its simplicity to remind me that before God, my character is exposed. I must look at the inner parts, the inmost places.

Clearly Defined

There are other pages to my prayer list that remind me of people and situations that need my prayers. No prayer is easy, but when I get to this page I must take a sober, gut-level look at who I am before God. It is a page entitled "character." Here I pray through the things in my character that need to change from weaknesses into strengths. As I pray through these things, I am reminded of the words in the song "Jesus Loves Me," "I am weak, but he is strong." Praying through them day after day forces me to rely on God and strengthens my faith as I have seen him answer my prayers time and time again.

Too often we stay generic in our prayers: "Help me be a better person, help me to change, to love you more, God..."

Too often we don't know specifically what we need to change and so don't have a clear aim in going after it. When we aim at nothing, that is what we hit. Can you put your character sins and weaknesses into words? Are they clearly defined in your mind? If they are not, it is unlikely you will be victorious in overcoming them.

In Touch with the Truth

We learn the truth about our character from the Word of God which discerns the thoughts and intentions of our heart (Hebrews 4:12-13). It is like a mirror reflecting how we look spiritually (James 1:23-25).

We also learn the truth about ourselves from other people in our lives (Proverbs 20:5). I remember years ago when I was a freshman in college and was given many new responsibilities of leadership. I was ambitious—part righteous, part selfish. I would read Philippians 2:3, "Do nothing out of *selfish* ambition," and see selfish thoughts in my heart hoping to "get credit for good deeds." I hated this in my heart and it dogged my feet. I remember crying out to God again and again, confessing to God what was there and begging him to take it away. I thought it would never leave me, but I took comfort in the scripture, "Resist the devil, and he will flee from you" (James 4:7). Finally, my character really began to change.

Several years ago I learned, through a relationship, how much deceit was in my character. I would stuff things I felt instead of saying what was in my heart. I could make something seem or sound better in my mind or with someone else. Openness and persistence in prayer, plus openness with other people has allowed my conscience to become very alert and tender in this area, so that I am able to change.

Partner to deceit in my character is fear—fear of conflict, fear of being vulnerable in my weakness, fear of God being against me, fear of heights, fear of fear... When someone shared with me one day that they didn't think I was a very "open" person, it bothered me deeply, but I didn't "get it." I didn't know how to change. I cried to God; I begged him to change me. I asked him to help me see it. I fasted; I went out to a quiet place for a day of prayer. Finally, I got it. I saw the fear and deceit and begged God to take it. I would talk about it with others and ask them how I was doing at being open and vulnerable. Today God has turned that weakness into a strength.

Keep Growing

Ask God to help you see what you need to change. Ask others what things they see in your sinful nature, those deep-rooted things that don't go away easily. What are they for you? Self-pity? Arrogance (self-reliance)? Timidity? A weak will? Bitterness? Being quick to quit? Lacking passion and fire for God? Lack of discipline? Maybe you have trouble getting on an emotional heart level with people or struggle with respecting your husband or loving your wife.

There are things I include in my prayers such as being on time, being more emotionally expressive to my husband and verbally appreciative for my friends. At times when I have felt stuck and lacked motivation, I have followed Philippians 2:13, "for it is God who works in you to will and to act..." I make myself stay and pray for the "want to" as well as the power. God has always been faithful. At times I've fasted and prayed or driven to my "special prayer places." I know several sisters who recently stayed up all night praying to change things in their character.

How badly do you want to change? It will show by the way you pray. Many times when I pray about changing my character I remind God (though I know he hasn't forgotten) of his promise in 2 Corinthians 12:9, "My power is made perfect in weakness." I picture in my mind's eye the weakness becoming a strength and how that would show itself practically in my life. That thought fires me up and gives me my goal. God, with all his unlimited means, will get me there. I can't quit until I'm there!

Prayer

My great and wonderful God and Father, I stand in awe as I think of the magnificent ways you have brought about change since the beginning. When all was void you spoke the world into existence. You changed a particle of dust into a human form and with your breath changed this form into man made in your image. From his rib you fashioned a woman and from this couple a child.

You changed an ocean into dry land, water into wine, five loaves and two fish into a feast that fed a multitude. You changed death into resurrection and eternal life. You changed timid, uneducated people into powerful, bold disciples, and persecutors into church leaders.

More recently Father, I have seen your hand at work in the winds of change. You have taken down the Iron Curtain, dismantled the Berlin Wall and undone South African apartheid. When you are in the picture, God, things change.

When I think of all your awesome deeds, and realize how faithless I can be when it comes to changing me, I am ashamed. Forgive me. I want to love like you love, care like you care, get disturbed when you are disturbed. . . to be like you more each day. I want to set the standard for my character that you have set in your Word.

God, help me to see the things I need to change and to have the humility, courage and perseverance to change. Turn my weaknesses into strengths so that my life can display the glory of your power and more people can come to know you.

Father, though you are the author of true change, thank you that you remain the same perfect, powerful and loving God yesterday, today and forever. I do believe that you can turn my weaknesses into strengths. Thank you so much. I love you with all of my heart.

Love, Jeanie

FOR FURTHER STUDY:

2 Corinthians 3:17-18
2 Peter 1:3-8
Philippians 2:12-13

21
The Church of Jesus

DOUG JACOBY
Scotland

And pray in the Spirit on all occasions with all kinds of prayers and requests. With this in mind, be alert and always keep on praying for all the saints (Ephesians 6:18).

God pleads with his people to *pray*, and the pages of his revelation to man are replete with the recorded prayers of his pleading people: people on the move or in dire straits or striving in some great undertaking; sometimes preparing to die, sometimes rejoicing that they are alive. There are Old Testament prayers for the nation, the city, the walls, the temple, the leaders and the safety of Israel; and above all, passionate prayers displaying the entire range of human emotions.

The Church of Jesus

Since the church (Greek *ekklesia*, or *assembly*) is the **body of Christ** on earth, the visible manifestation of the **kingdom of God**, and the full expression of the **family** God wills us to share in, disciples must have a deep commitment to pray for the needs of the church. We pray for the church "universal" (all congregations worldwide), the church "militant" (in her unceasing war against the forces of evil), and the church "triumphant" (as we accomplish the mission God has entrusted to us).

A Daunting Task

But praying for the saints is a daunting task! I remember well the late nights in summer 1985, on the verge of a special evangelistic effort to impact England, praying for *three hundred* campaign workers—most of whom I'd never met! What an effort—to say the worker's name and congregation, and strive to make some meaningful request! Have you tried to pray down *lists* of names? (The Lord blessed that campaign, I believe, because of prayer.)

Vain Repetitions

Am I a lazy dog if I don't pray every day for everyone in my own church or ministry? After all, Paul did say "*all* the saints." How can we avoid the cheap variety of one-line name mentioning, yet pray for everyone in the limited time God has given us? Surely, like me, you have felt guilty when a brother or sister said, "I'm praying for you"— when you knew in your heart that your efforts to pray for that person were minimal. Maybe you resolved to do better but it didn't really change.

We Need Help!

If you've ever struggled with any of these problems, then you'll appreciate input on how better to pray for the church of Jesus. Without prayer we forfeit the sense of family and the power God offers us, creating instead a sense of superficiality, guaranteeing a tepid, disunified response to the charge to "Go." We need help. Praying is *hard work*. Now let's get practical!

In Ephesians 6 Paul urges us to pray with variety, creativity, specificity and perseverance. Paul himself felt responsibility for all the churches (2 Corinthians 11:28) and prayed for all the disciples (Philippians 1:4). Since I became a disciple in 1977 I have changed my prayer strategy continuously. Some of my ideas have been winners (others, dead losers!). How many new ideas have you tried?

Practical Tips

Pray for upcoming meetings. Since church (*ekklesia*) means *assembly* (the exact same word you find in Acts 19:32), pray for everyone to be *assembled.* Pray for those not assembled, the organization of the meeting, the quality of singing, the impact on the visitors, and the conviction of the group. Pray for powerful meetings which empower the people of God for service.

Intercede for world leaders. God wants us to pray for our non-Christian leaders (1 Timothy 2:1-2). It helps to read the newspaper, watch the news, or subscribe to a news magazine. The few minutes a day you spend keeping up with world events will be well worth it. Pray for heads of state, politicians, royalty and opinion leaders by name.

Tour your city. Get a map of your metropolitan area. Now and again pray for regions and divisions, for Christian households and the unevangelized areas. Pray for God to bring visitors to church through *your* efforts from one of these unevangelized areas!

Incorporate biblical themes. Pray for the church in terms of the great themes of the Bible: God's faithfulness to his people, the remnant, the call to be radical, God's discipline of his people.

Tour the world. Sometimes I stand in front of my big world map and pray for the saints geographically. My map is mounted so that I can stick in colored pins wherever there are churches.

Pray for your elders, or to have elders. Churches need elders (Titus 1:5; Ephesians 4:11). Maybe your church doesn't yet have elders; pray for it to happen! This is God's plan and gives great stability and maturity to the church of Jesus. Pray for your staff and other leaders, too. And *tell* them you're praying for them!

Pray for the church's work among the needy of your city. The needs are endless. Helping the needy tenders our hearts and tells God and the world we want to follow Jesus in his love for people.

Pray for special ministries within your church. Pray for the children's program, the teaching program, international ministry, administrators and their wives, and new Bible discussion groups. In larger churches pray for special needs ministries to come together with qualified leaders: deaf ministry, substance abuse ministry, Vietnam veterans support group, arts ministry, athletes' outreach and so forth.

Pray for new church plantings. Every month a number of new churches are planted worldwide. Support them in prayer, tell your non-Christian friends about the frontiers being pushed back, and send the occasional letter or card of support.

These are some ideas that have worked for me. Some of them may make *your* prayers for the church more fresh, fulfilling, and even fun. Go to it!

Prayer

Dear God, we deeply desire to do your will and to take the message in this generation to every nation, every city, town and village. Our strength and resources are limited, but yours are unlimited. Give us your Spirit in a way that will shock us, move us, thrill us and keep us going. Do incredible things in our generation, and knit the worldwide brotherhood together; help us to meet our goals and always strive for excellence, even as Jesus gave his very best to accomplish the work that you gave him.

Many have tried to launch a spiritual revolution, a revolution that you are allowing us to see through your great power. Their hearts strayed, they tried and failed, and their movements have come to nothing. Halfhearted-ness and corruption destroyed their effectiveness and they fell woefully short. Please, Almighty Father, spare us that humiliation. Exalt your name and for your awesome glory use us to bring light and life to every corner of the earth.

Equip us at the local level with inspiring leaders and willing members. Multiply many times over our elderships, keep us from sin and compro-mise, let us wisely obey the laws of the land wherever we may work and remove any possible justification for calumny against your holy name. Give us a spirit of wisdom. Help us to preach the good news, heal the sick and help the poor, as our Master taught us.

We love the church bought with the precious blood of Jesus. Because of him, his cross, and in his name we are able to approach you. Amen.

FOR FURTHER STUDY:

Ephesians 3:14-21
Philippians 1:3-6
Colossians 1:3-12

22
The Harvest That Is Plentiful

BYRON PARSON

> Jesus went through all the towns and villages, teaching in their synagogues, preaching the good news of the kingdom and healing every disease and sickness. When he saw the crowds, he had compassion on them, because they were harassed and helpless, like sheep without a shepherd. Then he said to his disciples, "The harvest is plentiful but the workers are few. Ask the Lord of the harvest, therefore, to send out workers into his harvest field" (Matthew 9:35-38).

Jesus promises a great harvest. He declares that it is ready now. He does concede, however, that there is a problem. The workers are few. Though the Twelve are at his side, the workers are few. Earlier in Luke 6:17, a large crowd of "disciples" gathered to him, but still, the workers were few. In John 4:42 we read that an entire town listened to his words and concluded that he was the savior of the world. Yet Jesus maintains in Matthew 9:35 that the workers are few. The solution to the problem was simple: *Ask the Lord of the harvest* to send out workers.

God Controls the Harvest

As amazing as it may sound, our fruitfulness as individuals and congregations is limited primarily by one thing: God *himself*. He is the Lord of the harvest. He gives it, and he holds it back. John 1:13 reveals the source of the harvest. John says that those who received Jesus did so not because of human decision or a husband's will but rather, they were born of God. What, then, moves God to expand the size of his family on earth? Similarly, what would possibly compel him to limit new births into his family? Might it have something to do with the character of the workers and the kind of work they are doing? Jesus says to pray for workers, but what kind of workers does he have in mind? Consider the following contemporary parallel.

In the U.S., the government does not have the right to prevent couples from having children. It does however, reserve the right to take away children whose parents are found to be negligent. Not feeding, clothing and providing a safe environment for one's children is considered a crime. If parents do not have the means themselves, they are expected to ask for help and see to it that their children's needs are met. Likewise, in Luke 9:10-17 the disciples didn't personally have enough to meet the needs of 5,000 hungry men. But the Lord expected them to give what they had and ask God—PRAY—for whatever else was needed.

God is concerned, more than earthly fathers and governmental benefactors, about the physical welfare of his children. According to Matthew 6:27 he is concerned about what his children eat, drink and wear, in addition to what they believe and do.

Gratitude Controls the Harvesters

In Luke 9 Jesus called the Twelve to him and sent them on a limited commission. Their charge: 1) Preach the kingdom and 2) heal the sick (i.e. meet needs). They did this and drew crowds of thousands. Shortly thereafter, Jesus called the 72 to him and sent them out with the same instructions. Lastly, Jesus sent the faithful Eleven out with the great commission. Acts chapter 2 captures both what happened and, I believe, why the gospel spread so quickly:

> Everyone was filled with awe...all the believers were together and had everything in common...they gave to anyone as he had need...and ate together with glad and sincere hearts...enjoying the favor of all the people. And the Lord added to their number daily those who were being saved (Acts 2:43-47).

Acts 4:34 further asserts that there were no needy persons among them.

No wonder the number of disciples increased rapidly in Jerusalem. Who could keep from bragging about the incredible love God had shown them? Salvation wasn't just a doctrine or theology but rather a practical, tangible, measurable reality in their daily lives.

Peter's message at Pentecost began the new disciples' spiritual education. From there they studied daily at the feet of the apostles. They knew what to say. They knew they ought to say it. But what turned these converts into workers? Expectations? Accountability? Not according to the biblical record. It was the *help* they continued to receive in the kingdom. What will turn many more of our brothers and sisters into passionate workers for God? Every disciple seeing to it that there are no needy ones among us.

When Lauri and I sold most of our possessions and moved to Los Angeles some time back, we did so in faith. We were in the kingdom. God through the kingdom provided for so many of our physical needs. We stayed in the home of disciples as members of their family. We ate at their table with glad and sincere hearts. Over the years as a disciple I have received shoes, socks, slacks, shirts, ties, jackets, suits and coats. In the kingdom I often have been moved to tears by the kindness of God, expressed through the generosity of others. When my brother lay in intensive care in St. Louis awaiting a heart transplant, disciples of Jesus were there. Brothers pitched in at a moment's notice to help me get to my brother's side. This is what fuels a worker: gratitude. I can't help speaking about what I've seen and heard!

Jesus spent much of his time meeting physical needs, feeding, comforting, healing, serving. As a result, people spread the word even when strictly warned not to tell anyone (Mark 1:43-45). This reflects the power of meeting needs. This reflects the heart of a "worker."

We must believe that prayer is our most important tool in bringing the world to Jesus. We must pray for a harvest of biblical proportions, but we must, at the same time, seek to provide for people's needs the way Jesus provided for these needs. We must pray for the harvest by praying for workers who will serve like Jesus served.

To acquire a heart that puts others' needs before your own requires prayer. The strength to live this way, day in and day out, requires prayer. The trust needed to believe that the time, effort and money spent meeting those needs will end in a great harvest is developed in prayer. The supplies necessary to meet every need in the body must be acquired through prayer. The godliness to live as the Bible directs, whether we see a great harvest or not, requires prayer. So, let us pray.

Prayer

Dear Lord, your love and compassion are great. I praise you for the way you delight in not only meeting our needs but in giving us the desires of our hearts as well. Father, give me that heart. Help me to serve my brothers and sisters with the strength you provide. I pray to always give when it is in my power to do so.

Teach me, Lord, to love my neighbor as myself. I pray that among your children worldwide there be no needy one among us. Send out into the harvest field workers who overflow with gratitude.

For Further Study:

Ezekiel 34
Acts 6:1-7
2 Corinthians 9:6-15

23
Courage and Boldness

GUILLERMO ADAME
San Diego, California

"Be still, and know that I am God " (Psalm 46:10).

"Wow! You want *me* to be on the Bombay mission team?" Those words went through my head as I tried to remain calm back in July 1986. Feelings of excitement mixed with uncertainty filled my body. But it was fear that gripped me. Why? God had been preparing me for six years "to go anywhere, to do anything." I'm a disciple of Jesus. Right? I had already made it through the times when I first shared my faith, did my first personal Bible study with a non-Christian, led my first Bible discussion group, said my first public prayer and preached my first sermon. God had taught me so much about not being fearful and timid. But this was different! India was going to turn my whole life upside down. Everything was going to be new. New friends, new culture, new country. I *needed* to pray.

Fear is powerful. Most of us have felt its effects, but God can enable us to overcome fear and timidity and live boldly and courageously for him. Prayer reminds me God is in control, this is God's kingdom, and this is God's battle. I belong to God and God will make me successful. God will not let us be tempted beyond what we can bear (1 Corinthians 10:13). Prayer has always been comforting for me because I know that I am never alone. God is always with me, always watching, always taking care of me. "Be still, and know that I am God."

To pray our way through to courage and boldness, we need to focus on three areas.

Trust

> For God did not give us a spirit of timidity, but a spirit of power, of love and of self-discipline (2 Timothy 1:7).

We must understand we are exactly who God wants us to be. God will make up for whatever deficiency or weakness we have. His Spirit lives within us. We are his children. Once we understand this principle we will be much more bold and courageous in our confrontation of the everyday battles raging around us.

Evangelism intimidates many disciples. Many of us become insecure, feeling we lack the talent, knowledge or experience to do a good job in sharing our faith. We worry what another person will think of us. When these feelings occur, we must remember that we are God's instrument and are speaking God's words. God will give us exactly what to say and the victory will be ours.

My friend, Albert Shane, is an incredible example in this area. When Albert first became a Christian, he didn't have much education nor a great command of any language. He wasn't rich. He just loved God. He was grateful to be a Christian, and he wanted everyone to know what God had done for him. In just three short years, God has used Albert to help *hundreds* become disciples and today he serves as an evangelist in Cochin in Southern India. Albert is willing to trust God and his promises.

Righteousness

> The wicked man flees though no one pursues,
>   but the righteous are as bold as a lion (Proverbs 28:1).

According to Psalm 66:18, God will not hear us if we cherish sin in our hearts. Sin will stop us from praying to God and make us fearful and ineffective. God will create a pure heart in each of us if we are willing to ask (Psalm 51:10). Many disciples become deceived as to the condition of their hearts. The deception comes slowly over time. Having heard others affirm our hearts or having come through a great battle or having sacrificed something of great value for the kingdom, we get out of touch. Only God knows our hearts (Jeremiah 17:9). We must therefore, pray to God to reveal our hearts and to continue to test our motives (Proverbs 16:2).

Sin will cause us to become complacent, critical, callous and casual. The righteous are as bold as a lion and only God can make us righteous. "If we confess our sins, he is faithful and just and will forgive us our sins and purify us from all unrighteousness" (1 John 1:9).

Action
Do not merely listen to the Word, and so deceive yourselves. Do what it says (James 1:22).

Keep praying until you act. Keep praying until you succeed. The fear of failing is what stops most of us from being bold. Fear makes the cowardly slaves while the brave master fear. We will all fail many times during our lifetimes. The key to success is to continue to obey God. God promises us in Psalm 112:8 that a righteous man will have his "heart secure, he will have no fear; in the end he will look in triumph on his foes." If we truly believe in God and trust him, then we will follow his commands. The question that we must ask ourselves is, does our faith come from our results or our results from our faith?

Mark and Nadine Templer have labored in India for six years. Forced by persecution to leave India in 1990, they departed with a sense of failure, but returned in just one year's time with a renewed faith that God would do great things. Since their return God has multiplied the Indian churches from four to ten, and has raised up Indian nationals to lead in nine of the churches. The Templers are people who pray and refuse to give up.

God's work cannot be done in this world without courage. As disciples, we are going against the grain, upsetting the status quo and calling people to make serious changes. What we have to say will be rejected more often than welcomed. Boldness is required. We won't evangelize this world without it. We must have: *trust* that God will always be with us, *righteousness* that imitates Jesus, and *the desire to work* with all our hearts. "But we are not of those who shrink back and are destroyed, but of those who believe and are saved" (Hebrews 10:39).

"Wow! You want me to..."

Prayer

Dear Father, you are great in all that you have done and will do. You have made the earth as your footstool and there is nothing that you cannot do. No situation that cannot be changed, no heart that cannot be turned, no battle that cannot be won. Thank you, Lord, for saving me from the empty life that I was living and from the even bigger mistakes that I was going to make.

Father, you have always taken care of me and have given me the desires of my heart. You have always answered my prayers. My prayer now is for boldness. Allow me not to think of myself and my desires. I want to give 100 percent to you in everything I do and I am—in my speech, my actions, my mind and my life. Help me to speak boldly and confidently. Give me the exact words to say and give me the strength to make the most of every opportunity that you give to me. I don't want to live for my glory, Father, but for yours.

Let me not rely nor glory in past victories, but give me new victories every day. Help me in my unbelief so that my faith may grow stronger every day. I am grateful to be called your son and that you have chosen me from among the billions to be able to respond to your call. Use me in any way, as you see fit. I am always yours. I love you with all of my heart! In Jesus name, Amen.

FOR FURTHER STUDY:

Judges 6-7
1 Samuel 17
Matthew 14:22-32

24
Direction for Decisions

BRIAN SCANLON

And this is my prayer: that your love may abound more and more in knowledge and depth of insight, *so that you may be able to discern what is best* and may be pure and blameless until the day of Christ, filled with the fruit of righteousness that comes through Jesus Christ— to the glory and praise of God (Philippians 1:9-11 emphasis added).

Life is a parade of decisions. Some very important decisions: Should I accept that new job offer? Should I ask her to marry me? Other slightly less important decisions: What should I eat for dinner tonight? What movie should we see? For most, the parade becomes worrisome and wearisome. Even for the disciple of Jesus, decision making is not always easy. When we decided to make Jesus Lord of our lives, we decided to always do what Jesus would do—usually easier said than done and sometimes not easy to figure out. The most difficult decisions are not so much a question of right or wrong, but rather of what is good, better or best. Yet, as Christians, we can have ever increasing confidence in our ability to "discern what is best," thanks to our confidence in God and in spiritual men and women he has placed in our lives.

Confidence in God

Nobody knows the will of God better than God himself! Nobody wants you to know the will of God more than God himself! "This is the confidence we have in approaching God: that if we ask anything according to his will, he hears us. And we know that if he hears us—whatever we ask—we know that we have what we asked of him" (1 John 5:14-15). Asking God for wisdom to understand his will *is according to his will!* "For the Lord gives wisdom, and from his mouth come knowledge and understanding" (Proverbs 2:6). First of all, God gives wisdom through prayer. "If any of you lacks wisdom, he should ask God, who gives generously to all without finding fault, and it will be given" (James 1:5). Did you get that? Wisdom generously given to you! "But when he asks, he must believe and not doubt" (vs. 6). We simply need to believe it!

Second, God gives wisdom through his Word, to those "who by constant use have trained themselves to distinguish between good and evil" (Hebrews 5:14). We must train ourselves through constant study of the Word to be able to make good spiritual decisions. It's at this point that we often make too great a distinction between prayer and Bible study. When faced with an important decision or a situation I don't know how to handle, I have learned the value of getting away with my Bible, meditating on pertinent passages, and praying for God to give me insight and understanding. Decision-making can be exhilarating rather than overwhelming. This is the confidence we can and must have in approaching God: *He will give us wisdom to discern what is best.*

Confidence in the Family of God

God has been giving wisdom to men and women in his kingdom long before we personally began asking. It would be foolishly arrogant not to actively seek out this wisdom God has made available to each of us in the body of Christ! "Remember your leaders who spoke the Word of God to you. Consider the outcome of their way of life and imitate their faith" (Hebrews 13:7). Leaders in the kingdom of God are simply people we can trust and respect. Though far from perfect, we can respect the lives they have built through years of solid spiritual decisions. We can trust their sincere desire to guide us as they continue to speak the Word of God to us. We should pray continually that God grants them greater wisdom and insight to impart to others.

I remember my decision to move to France to work with the church in Paris. I knew well Matthew 28:18-20. I had been praying to God concerning my future. I consistently prayed for the wisdom of the spiritual leaders in my life. I trusted their desire to do what was best and respected their discernment in the situation. And God has since blessed that decision beyond my wildest dreams!

In the end, we have to make our own decisions and take responsibility for them. It's too easy to wait passively for something to happen and then call it the will of God or to just let someone else tell us what to do. Paul's words in Romans 12 give us some vital principles:

> Therefore, I urge you, brothers, in view of God's mercy, to offer your bodies as living sacrifices, holy and pleasing to God—this is your spiritual act of worship. Do not conform any longer to the pattern of this world, but be transformed by the renewing of your mind. Then you will be able to test and approve what God's will is—his good, pleasing and perfect will (Romans 12:1-2).

We can be confident about discerning the will of God when we have first offered ourselves to God as living sacrifices—when we have put ourselves on the altar and surrendered our wills. We may wrestle with God in prayer, as Jesus did (Matthew 26:36). But once we have wrestled with God, asked for wisdom, and have talked with other people we trust, we can make decisions with confidence that God has given us the wisdom we needed. Then, whatever the result, we can be confident that "in all things God works for the good of those who love him..." (Romans 8:28).

Prayer

Father in Heaven, how good, pleasing and perfect your will is! You've made it clear that, above all, you want every man to be saved as he comes to a knowledge of the truth. I thank you and praise you for giving me the opportunity to respond to the truth and to know you. Open my heart that I might be able to know you better and give me wisdom to better help others to come to know you. In your infinite knowledge and perfect wisdom, I ask you to give me deeper insight into the needs of others and greater discernment as to how to meet those needs.

As I meditate on your Word, fill my mind with your thoughts and pour your heart into mine, that I might think and act in every situation as you want me to. I praise you and thank you for the people you have put in my life to guide and counsel me. I pray that you will continue to give them ever-increasing wisdom as you work through them to help me discern what is best. (Pray specifically for certain people of influence in your life).

Father, at this very moment there are many decisions I need to make, and I know that no decision is without significance in your sight. In each situation, make clear to me all that I should consider, and give me wisdom to discern what is best. (Pray specifically for each situation and decision to be made).

Father, thank you for the confidence I have that you love me, that you have heard me, and that you will enable me to make the best decisions for you.

For Further Study:

Psalm 25:1-8
Psalm 73:21-26
Proverbs 4:1-13

25
Power for our Weakness

STEVE BROWN
Nashville, Tennessee

> To keep me from becoming conceited because of these surpassingly great revelations, there was given me a thorn in my flesh, a messenger of Satan, to torment me. Three times I pleaded with the Lord to take it away from me. But he said to me, "My grace is sufficient for you, for my power is made perfect in weakness." Therefore I will boast all the more gladly about my weaknesses, so that Christ's power may rest on me. That is why, for Christ's sake, I delight in weaknesses, in insults, in hardships, in persecutions, in difficulties. For when I am weak, then I am strong (2 Corinthians 12:7-10).

On January 31 I hit the winning jumper in a spirited warm-up game for our church basketball league in Dallas. Pretty good for an elder in the church. *I was feelin' good about myself!* The next day, as I was doing some paper work at the office after a ministry staff meeting, my left side began to feel numb. I tried to ignore it, but within minutes I had little use of my arm and leg and the left side of my mouth had begun to droop. The paramedics were called. My wife and I exchanged a look that said, "This must be the big one," since I've had high blood pressure for years and my family history is straight out of the high risk textbook for vascular problems. The taste of the previous night's victory was quickly forgotten—that sense of self-importance was totally obscured.

Before the paramedics could arrive I felt the strength begin to return. You can imagine the joyful chorus of emotions that ran through me. "Man! That was a close one! Just a fluke, I guess. Now, I can walk on my own."

But it wasn't to be. Later that night, after a severe attack, I was hospitalized, and by Thursday I was totally paralyzed on my left side. Lying on that hospital bed, I thought so many things, not the least of which was "I may never shoot hoops again!" I couldn't even think about our four kids without breaking into tears.

I thought about all the plans we had for making an impact in Texas. In short, many things that I had relied upon for my self-worth had been ripped away. Six weeks later I was rolled out of the hospital in a wheelchair. The doctors decided that my paralysis was due to multiple sclerosis (MS). It was a shocking introduction to weakness, and the beginning of a struggle to understand what God was doing and what he wanted me to learn.

I had become weak. And I thought of Paul's words in 2 Corinthians 12, "For when I am weak, then I am strong."

What is Weakness?

When Paul refers to weakness in this passage, his definition is very broad. He uses the same Greek word in a variety of ways in other contexts: physical sickness (Philippians 2:26), weakness of faith (Romans 14:1-2), and a weak conscience (1 Corinthians 8:11,12). Here he seems to include physical difficulties, persecution and even emotional struggles. The meaning of his famous reference to the "thorn in the flesh" is disputed, but bottom line, it doesn't matter. The nature or even the degree of the weakness is not the point. *His point is that if you are not aware of your weaknesses, then God cannot make you strong!*

I learned quickly that simple tasks like tying shoes, buttoning shirts and tying a tie made me break out in sweat as much as running the length of the court had before. I was dependent on a nurse, or more often than not, my wife, Diane, for the most elementary daily activities. Most of you don't have MS and perhaps are not physically challenged in any way, but if you fail to see your own disability—your weakness—then you will not depend on God. Thus, Paul says God had to make him weak so that he was forced to depend on God. Of course, I could have refused help and gone around with my shoes untied, and my shirt unbuttoned, but that would be stupid. How much more stupid is it when we go around spiritually deficient because we fail to get help from God?

Boasting in Weakness

Recognizing my weakness was one thing. Dealing with it was another story. A riot of different feelings accompanied my newfound weakness—none of which led me to boast about it! Paul was able to look back and see the great impact for God his weakness had brought about. Now, 12 months later, I, too, can look back and see some of the great things God has done through my illness. One of my first caretakers was a physical therapist who subsequently became a disciple. My weakness lets God shine!

All-Sufficient Grace

Paul's next lesson is that "grace is sufficient." It is enough. It is all that I need. My sinful nature wants all the ego strokes—to be respected, to be influential, to be useful. But God wants me to understand that his grace is all I need. Even though I can't do as much as I did before physically, out of my struggle with MS has come an intense conviction that God will give me the strength to accomplish what he wants me to do each day. My problems come when I get busy with what I think I should do. Praise God, his grace covers those times! I blow it and he forgives me. Tomorrow we start over.

The Role of Prayer

I won't forget the day that my doctor and Diane came into the hospital room and panicked to find me on the floor. They hurried to my side probably thinking CPR was in order. But I had managed to get out of my bed and onto the floor, purposely putting myself in the position that God had wanted me in all along. I admitted the truth. My heart had been in headlong rebellion telling me, "I can do something." But what was really needed was the same posture as Jesus when he said, "By myself I can do nothing." That's when weakness came along to teach me without God sustaining my life and giving me breath, I would be dead.

Prayer is simply the key that unlocks the door to God's free reign in our lives. He reigns whether we like it or not, but he will not take away our will. We have to surrender it. If you read this chapter looking for the key to praying away your weaknesses, whether it be sickness or persecution or family troubles, then you will be disappointed. Getting rid of the weakness is not the point (although there's nothing wrong with that—Paul prayed for it three times). The key is to humbly submit yourself to God, depending on his power and relying on his strength, so he can use you as he sees fit. Then we can all say with Paul, "When I am weak, then I am strong."

Prayer

O God, without you I am so weak, so helpless.
I can do nothing. Nothing at all.
But by your grace
I live. I move. I breathe.
Thank You!
Thank you for life, for opportunities, for Today.
Today Lord,
Overcome my weakness by your power.
Give me the strength I need to do what you want me to.
And may my "to do list" be the same as yours!
Help me not to squander that strength selfishly, foolishly,
But to use it
for you.
for the kingdom.
And may all the glory be yours!
In Jesus' name. Amen.

FOR FURTHER STUDY:

Psalm 44: 3-8
2 Corinthians 13:3-4
Hebrews 4:14-15

26
Friends and Loved Ones

LAVONIA DRABOT
Charlotte North Carolina

And the prayer offered in faith will make the sick person well; the Lord will raise him up. If he has sinned he will be forgiven. Therefore, confess your sins to each another and pray for each another so that you may be healed. The prayer of a righteous man is powerful and effective (James 5:15-16).

In the dark. On their knees. Silently and aloud. People have prayed for each of us—both before and after we became Christians. God worked in those prayers to soften our hearts and expose our sin, to lead us to repentance. Once we were forgiven and healed, we began to pray for others. The cycle of intercessory prayer. The multiplying principle. Each one passes on the blessing he has received. To intercede or pray on someone else's behalf is a privilege. We approach the God of the universe and he hears us. Our prayers are sacrifices which are pleasing to him (Hebrews 13:15).

Expand Your View

We know that God wants us to pray for people, but we need to remember why. God desires our family members to be saved more than we do, and prayer helps us to see them as God does. God also wants the heart of each disciple to continue to change into the likeness of Jesus. It is amazing to see how our praying for the people in our lives can move God to soften hearts and remove obstacles.

In reading Paul's letters, I saw his deep affection for the disciples in each church he had influence over: "I want you to know how much I am struggling for you...and for all who have not met me personally" (Colossians 2:1). Who do you struggle for? Family?

Friends? Neighbors? That's good and right. But do you pray for people you have never even met? Probably not. I encourage you to study Paul's letters and gain conviction about the specificity of his prayers. Paul's heart ached for men and women he did not even know! What better expression of our love than prayer!

When Ron and I first moved to Chicago, we prayed diligently that we would meet someone who would become a disciple. After several months, we moved again and reached out to our new neighbors that first weekend. Eddie and Barbette were baptized into Christ within three weeks! Their decision did not come without much struggle and challenge, though, and Ron and I continued to pray for them to make it into the kingdom. We struggled in prayer at each decision point (Philippians 1:10). God blessed our prayers and our persistence in a great way!

Something that has been extremely fulfilling in my prayer times recently has been praying for each of the disciples in the Midwest family of churches by name. At the Midwest Jubilee in September, Ron and I asked the disciples to fill out a prayer request card if they wanted us to pray for their specific needs. About 3,000 responded. I was so moved by the humility and openness of the people. The needs were heart-felt and acute: tragic deaths of family members; children or spouses who'd fallen away from God; difficulties in connecting with God and other people. Praying for these people has sensitized me to the needs of the individuals Ron and I lead. I feel bonded to people I don't even know. And now, it is so exciting when we visit the Midwest churches to be able to put names and faces together; the Holy Spirit has been faithful in helping us to remember those we have been praying for!

Where are the limits in your prayer life? Take inspiration from Paul and expand your view! "As for me, far be it from me that I should sin against the Lord by failing to pray for you," said Samuel to King Saul (1 Samuel 12:23). When we fail to pray for the people and needs God prompts us to, we sin. Pray for the leaders in other areas of the church, not just those directly in your region. Pray for ministries in different parts of the world, for their leaders, their finances, their faith. Pray not only for the various nations but for the individuals in them who need to be saved. Prayer will put faces on this lost world and move you to be more focused on your purpose even as it moves God to work.

Jesus Is Our Intercessor

I think that sometimes we fail to pray with as much fervor or confidence as we should because we are painfully aware of our own inadequacies. Every time we pray, we need to thank God that his power is not limited by our weakness.

> ...the Spirit helps us in our weakness. We do not know what we ought to pray for, but the Spirit himself intercedes for us with groans that words cannot express (Romans 8:26).

> Christ Jesus...is at the right hand of God and is also interceding for us (Romans 8:34).

We have every reason to be confident in approaching God when we know that "my intercessor is my friend as my eyes pour out tears to God; on behalf of a man he pleads with God as a man pleads for his friend" (Job 16:20-21). A friend is an incredible blessing. A friend is loyal, speaks the truth in love, builds you up when you are down, is always there when you are in need, and makes you look good in spite of all your weaknesses. In other words, a friend complements you by adding what is missing. No matter how inadequate we feel before God, Jesus makes us complete in God's sight. It is good to visualize Jesus and the Holy Spirit working on our behalf. Jesus is the loyal friend, speaking the truth through his Word, and inspiring us to trust God. When the prayers won't flow or we feel as if we are not connecting, we know that Jesus and the Holy Spirit are searching our hearts and taking our requests before God. Our confidence comes not from ourselves but from the knowledge that Jesus loves us and intercedes with the Holy Spirit on our behalf.

Realizing how desperately we need Jesus to intercede for us should remind us how much others need us to go before God on their behalf.

Prayer

Dear Father, my God, my protector, my salvation, my friend, I pray that, in your great power through the Holy Spirit, you would please help me to have people on my heart. I want to specifically know the needs of my friends and family in order to petition you effectively on their behalf. I pray that out of your glorious riches you would strengthen them in their inner being so that Christ would dwell in their hearts through faith.

I pray that they will be rooted and established in love to grasp how wide and long and high and deep is the love of Christ, so that they will be filled to the measure of all the fullness of you. I pray for them to have a spirit of wisdom and revelation so that they may know you better and that the eyes of their hearts may be enlightened in order that they may know the hope to which you have called them.

I pray that they will know you, the only true God, and that they will understand and be impacted by the cross of Jesus, your son. Father, I am so grateful for the women you have put in my life to show me the truth about myself. Thank you for their love, patience and belief in me. Help me to do the same for others.

FOR FURTHER STUDY:

Ephesians 3:14-19
Colossians 1:9-12
2 Thessalonians 1:11-12
James 5:16

27
Enemies and Opposition

JOHN PORTER
Clemson, South Carolina

"Love your enemies and pray for those who persecute you" (Matthew 5:44).

It was one of those appointments that I was not looking forward to. A brother in the church I was leading had become bitter and resentful towards the church and towards me personally. As we sat down to talk, the brother pulled out his "record of wrongs" of what seemed like every sin I had committed in the last two years (some real and some imagined). I found out that the brother had not only directed his negative attitudes towards me, but that he had also been lying to and poisoning the thoughts of other Christians. It was extremely painful to realize that a dear brother to whom we had opened our home and our hearts was now attacking us.

Fire from Heaven?

Unfortunately, what began as pain quickly turned to rage. Every fiber in my body wanted to explode. I knew that the true root of his anger was an impure dating relationship that my wife, Barbara, and I were discouraging. This was not a weak individual who needed help. This was an embittered opponent of the leadership, the church, and the biblical stance we were taking. I felt like James and John did when they wanted to call fire down from heaven to destroy a Samaritan village. "The church—and even the world—would be better off without this person!" I insisted to myself.

A short while later, in spite of our prayers and efforts, the brother managed to spread his bitterness to the sister he was dating, and she left the church with him to pursue their relationship. Soon thereafter, they were married. There was nothing else we could do. We turned desperately to God. We prayed that the couple would "wake up" and realize how much they had hurt God and themselves. We prayed for their brokenness and restoration to God's kingdom.

I am convicted to realize, in retrospect, that we cried out to God much more fervently on behalf of the sister than of the brother. Although we understood that she had made her own choice to leave God, we also knew that she had been greatly weakened by the brother's negative influence and had fallen prey to Satan's scheme. She seemed to be much more a "victim" than a "perpetrator." Nevertheless, we now understand that it is in just such circumstances that Jesus' exhortation to pray for our enemies takes on a deeper meaning.

Glaringly Different

Undoubtedly, many people have had enemies more intense and brutal than ours. Opposition may take the form of critical brothers, angry family members, deceptive journalists, or even, as Jesus himself could attest to, murderers. But whoever the enemies may be, the words of Jesus are still the same: "Love your enemies and pray for those who persecute you" (Matthew 5:44).

As disciples of Jesus Christ, we are called to be glaringly different from those around us. Living in a "religious" part of the world where people are apparently "good" can make this challenging at times. Ironically, it is our enemies who afford us the opportunity to glorify God by shining like stars in the universe (Philippians 2:15). Perhaps in no other area can a Christian so obviously distinguish himself from the religious "do-gooders." To forgive, love and pray for our enemies is behavior described in the Bible as "perfect" (Matthew 5:48) that is, like God. To be "like God" is to go completely "against the grain" of our sinful human nature. Only someone who loves God earnestly and has an eternal perspective on life is able to surrender himself to this depth of love.

We must also understand that this behavior is neither optional nor outstanding—it is standard operating procedure for every disciple. The Bible emphatically states that we must forgive and love our enemies to be permitted to be sons of God and to enter heaven (Matthew 5:44; 18:35).

God's answer to opposition is not humanistic retaliation but love and prayer. The keys to "righteous" prayers in these situations are, of course, found in the Scriptures. When praying for our enemies we should focus on:

1. Their need for forgiveness and salvation (Luke 23:34; Acts 7:60)
2. The power of God to change them and the situation (Acts 4:24-28)
3. Our need to continue to preach boldly (Acts 4:29)

These will produce a quiet confidence that God is in control and will use the situation to bear much fruit and give glory to his name.

Barbara and I are thrilled to report that after more than a year of prayer (and a move to another city) we received a call that our "enemy" and his wife wanted to return to the church. The Christians began to reach out to them. In time, their genuine brokenness and repentance was evident to all, and they were restored to the fellowship. They are now fruitful and zealous disciples!

Love for our enemies unleashes a power unlike any other. Think of how many lives have been changed more than the centuries by the example of Jesus loving and forgiving his persecutors while hanging on a cross! I am thankful that God gives us the strength to "go against the grain" and love and pray for our enemies. Against a backdrop of anger, hate and despair, how brightly we, as disciples, can shine as a result of this simple but powerful solution to opposition!

Prayer

Sovereign Lord, we come before you now thanking you because you are in total control. We praise you because you alone have absolute authority over every disaster and difficulty, big or small. We exalt you because you opened the Red Sea, shut the mouths of lions, raised people from the dead and have advanced your kingdom throughout the ages. We kneel before you now, acknowledging your perfect plan in all of the present difficulties that we now face.

Father, we ask that these trials would not become the focus of our lives but that our hearts would be dominated by thoughts of your power, love and divine plan. We thank you for these challenges because we recognize how prideful and independent we are, and we know that without challenges, we would not have the depth in our relationship with you that we so desperately need.

Father, we ask that you would forgive our enemies for all of the opposition that we are receiving. We ask for the strength to love our enemies, and we pray that your power and love would lead them to a relationship with you.

Father, give us the foresight and love to preach your Word boldly and confidently, in spite of our trials, so that your kingdom will spread and your Holy Name will be lifted up all over our community and the world. All of this we pray in the name of Jesus, the perfect example of love in the face of persecution. Amen.

For Further Study:

Matthew 5:44
Luke 6:34-35
Romans 12:14
1 Peter 4:12-17

THE
DIFFERENCE
IT MAKES

*More accounts from those
who have launched out by faith and have
seen how faithful God is*

28
Going Through the Open Door

ANDREW FLEMING

"So I say to you: Ask and it will be given to you; seek and you will find; knock and the door will be opened to you. For everyone who asks receives; he who seeks finds; and to him who knocks, the door will be opened" (Luke 11:9-10).

Instead of understanding "asking," "seeking" and "knocking" as three separate commands to be obeyed, it is best to understand them as three steps towards a single goal—taking an opportunity afforded us by God. The idea of a door being opened is associated with a God-given opportunity (1 Corinthians 2:12), and as we pray, we need to be alert to what opportunities for faith and action God is trying to make clear to us. In the past 11 years since my baptism into Christ, I have seen God move in many incredible ways, but never so amazingly as in his opening of the door to the former Soviet Union.

Prayer Is Dangerous

One evening in the summer of 1984, I was praying for the work of the Boston church where I had become a disciple nine months earlier. As I used the telephone list of leaders on the back of the church bulletin to guide my prayers, I came to the name of the leader of the Stockholm mission team, who I knew had spent the past nine months looking for a co-worker to go with him on a language internship to Sweden. I remember wondering in prayer to God, "Why has no one been found? Why doesn't anyone want to go? Sweden is a great country. Stockholm is a beautiful city." and then, "No!...No!...I don't want to go!" *But it was too late.*

I had read in Ezekiel 22:30 earlier that day describing how God looked for someone to build up the wall and stand in the gap but found no one. Although many around me had been asked, the leadership had never personally approached me (I had only been a ministry intern for six months and really had my heart set on going on a third-world mission team). I couldn't finish that prayer until I had promised God that I would bring it up to the elders the next day at a staff meeting. They reacted with excitement because a few weeks earlier they had decided to stop looking and interviewing for this "helper" and simply began praying that God would put it on someone's heart. Within three weeks, I was in Sweden and was studying Swedish, and because of various circumstances, became the leader of the team!

The Russians Are Waiting

Just before leaving for Stockholm, I went out and bought a map of Scandinavia because I wanted to pray for the different cities of those countries (and my world geography needed a little help). I remember opening the map and finding Stockholm, Oslo, Copenhagen and Helsinki and praying for them. But something caught my eye in the lower right-hand margin. There was a cut into the margin so that a city of Russia could be included on the map (and even more importantly, included in my prayer)—*Moscow!* At that moment, I began to pray for the first time to play a part in the evangelization of Russia. During the next few years I would speak about these dreams during world missions seminars and at conferences for Soviet missions hosted by the young Stockholm church.

Around the same time that the Stockholm church was planted (1986), the Communist party of the USSR introduced programs of *glasnost* (openness) and *perestroika* (reconstruction). These political changes exposed the weakest face of the Soviet regime in 70 years, causing both their political power and support to waver at home. The prayers of the saints were going up to God all over the world, and not surprisingly, soon after a day of specific prayer at the 1989 World Missions Seminar, the Berlin wall fell. These events led to the decision by kingdom leaders to plant the Moscow church in the summer of 1991 and my wife, Tammy, and I were asked to lead the planting. It was a dream come true and a prayer answered!

A Righteous Friend with Connections in High Places

Meanwhile in Copenhagen, Denmark, Chris Reed, the evangelist there, a good friend and a former member of the Stockholm team, was praying to convert a Russian man who could be my right hand in the Russian work. The next day as Chris was out sharing his faith, he noticed a 6'5" man standing on the train platform. Chris sized him up as the most intimidating person there and went up and offered him a invitation to Bible discussion. The not-very-talkative fellow turned out to be a top physics student from Moscow doing one year's special study in Copenhagen.

Chris was so excited that it was only after the train pulled away with the Russian standing there looking back through the window that he realized he had not gotten his phone number and address. But Chris prayed and the Spirit of God prevailed. Misha Rakovshik came on his own to the Bible discussion, studied the Bible, became a disciple, and by July 1 was home in Moscow awaiting the arrival of the mission team.

Misha became my translator; after eight months he was preaching on his own; by the next summer he had become an evangelist. Today, he and his wife, Sasha, lead the Moscow Church of Christ which has 1900 members and Sunday attendance of almost 3,000 at this writing! Prayer is powerful in the hands of people who love God! In the former Soviet Union we presently have 12 churches in five republics with more than 5,000 disciples and a plan of *openness* and *reconstruction* for the remaining 10 republics by the end of 1997.

God has plans and dreams for our lives which are even greater than our own. As we pray we should not only seek to understand our will and what we want, but to ask questions and listen to what God wants for our lives. God can do more than we can ask and imagine—and to God be the glory.

Prayer

Dear Father in heaven, thank you so much for the privilege of being your disciples and children. Thank you for your continual love that desires and hopes incredible things for our lives. Thank you for Jesus and the way in which he has shown us how to live and think and walk before you here on earth.

Thank you for the natural world which so powerfully declares your strength and character as we live out our lives. Thank you, Father, for the way you have been moving in your kingdom and allowed us not only to experience your mercy and your grace, but also to lead others to them. As you rule the nations, give us the conviction to administer your love!

Forgive us, Father, for those times we think that we know so much about your will that we forget to ask and we forget to listen. Remind us to continually seek deeper insight into your Word and deeper understanding into your purposes for our lives. Remind us to listen to our own words and learn about our own hearts so that sin will not deceive us. Remind us of the simple decision we made in the beginning to be your disciples and seek your kingdom first.

Thank you, Father, for the gift of your Spirit, and help each one of us to fan into flame the living fire that you have placed in each one of us. Use our lives to display your character and heart.

We love you, and thank you, and pray to you in Jesus' name, Amen!

FOR FURTHER STUDY:

Colossians 4
Revelation 3:7-13
Acts 16

29
Plans to Prosper Us

FLAVIO AND RENEE URIBE

"I will come to you and fulfill my gracious promise to bring you back to this place. For I know the plans I have for you," declares the Lord, "plans to prosper you and not to harm you, plans to give you hope and a future. Then you will call upon me and come and pray to me, and I will listen to you. You will seek me and find me when you seek me with all your heart" (Jeremiah 29:10b-13).

Prayer is what has made the difference in our lives and in the church in Bogotá, Colombia. The church began in April 1992, with 10 disciples (three Americans and seven Colombians). We arrived during the middle of a time of electricity rationing and a telephone workers' strike, which meant we had no contact with any other country, and we could not receive any money. But we prayed to God, and he gave us a great beginning. In the first two months, we grew by 30 and in the first eight months, by 100.

God continually calls us to our knees. The toughest time for the church was five months after the planting; the church leaders, Peter and Laura Garcia-Bengochea, were needed to assume the leadership of the church in Mexico City. This was a major test of our faith: our "parents" in the faith were leaving! My girlfriend and I were left to fill the gap. In spite of all the transition, no one left the faith, and the church has marched on. As of this writing, there are now 250 disciples in Bogotá.

God's Protection

It is always amazing how God answers our specific prayers: keeping the disciples safe in such an unsafe city, being personally fruitful, and raising up leaders. For instance, in 1993 we had a car-bomb explode two blocks away from our apartment, but we were not harmed in any way. Within days, another car-bomb exploded downtown where several Christians have businesses only a block away, and yet, none of them were hurt. In becoming disciples, many have turned away from the business of drug trafficking, but there have been no harmful attacks on individuals or the church by the drug cartels.

God wants us to be personally fruitful and loves to answer our prayers about being effective in the ministry. Recently, in a period of less than six months, I was able to personally meet, study the Bible with and baptize three very talented university students.

The growth of the church in Bogotá has brought a great need for leaders. We have come before God time after time with this need. God has brought so many talented, dynamic people into the church and given them a big heart for people and for the kingdom. In our church, except for us, there are no leaders older than two and a half years in the faith. Several people have begun to lead Bible discussion groups within a month of their conversions!

Benjamin is an example of the many Colombian disciples who are not only enjoying their Christianity, but also taking responsibility for the evangelization of their homeland. When he was merely three months old in the faith, he became a ministry intern.

His Timing Is Perfect

God does not always answer our prayers immediately. I began to pray for the evangelization of my country when I became a Christian in Orlando, Florida, in 1988. In 1989 I left a well-paying job as an electrical engineer and moved to Mexico City to prepare to be a part of the Bogotá mission team. I was not offered a job in the ministry right away, so I took a job teaching history at a bilingual school. I spent three years praying, waiting to go back to my native land.

As a single in the church, I found that one of the hardest areas to trust God in is in romance, but I prayed and believed. It wasn't until I was in Colombia that years of praying were answered. I started dating the kind of woman I had always dreamed and prayed I would marry—Renee Rheinbolt. She had already spent five years as a missionary in Mexico City, and had wondered if she would end her life fruitful, but alone. God put us on the same mission team and took care of everything! It wasn't long before we were married, leading the church, eventually being appointed evangelist and women's ministry leader.

Praying our marriage would bring more glory to God, we saw much fruit in the ministry in our first month as a married couple. There were challenges—the closest mature married couple who could give us input was three and a half hours away *by plane*. But we prayed, and God has taught us how to resolve conflicts quickly. We have no doubts—prayer has made the difference.

We have learned throughout the years that we must keep praying even during the dark weeks, months and years, when it seems, because of lack of results, that prayer is wasted time. We believe God is always listening, but he is putting the messages "on hold," waiting for the perfect time, after he has taught us a thing or two. A life built by prayer is a solid life, but the life built on worry and self-reliance will be unfruitful, insecure and unhappy.

We are very thankful to God for listening to all of our prayers!

Prayer

Dearest God, you are such a great God with so much power. Your love is overwhelming. It is incredible how intimately you are involved in our lives. We are so thankful you want this world evangelized and you have chosen us to participate. Every day the kingdom grows and expands. We beg you to please evangelize the world in this generation. Help us always to keep a global perspective and not narrow our vision only to our own personal ministry.

Dearest Lord, in Latin America there are still 460,000,000 people who need you so deeply. God, their lives are so empty. Instead of being full of you, they are full of hurt and sadness, as a result of their broken marriages, abortions, sexual abuse, incest, corruption and violence.

Please, God, help us to love those around us with a deeper compassion and to feel their pain. We need you so much; we are nothing without you. Only you are making a difference in this world and will continue to make a difference. We want to be completely filled with you and to imitate your heart more and more every day.

Thank you for listening and caring. We love you so very much. In Jesus' name, Amen.

FOR FURTHER STUDY:

1 Corinthians 13:13
Colossians 1:3-6
1 Thessalonians 1:3

30
Warriors Who Will Change the World

JOHN CAUSEY

This is the confidence we have...that if we ask anything according to his will, he hears us. And if we know that he hears us—whatever we ask—we know that we have what we asked of him (1 John 5:14-15).

The basic difference between an ordinary man and a warrior is that a warrior takes everything as a challenge, while an ordinary man takes everything either as a blessing or a curse!

As disciples, what we are on the inside is the real measure of who we are—whether a person of prayer, deep conviction and spiritual insight or an empty shell waiting for the blessings of God to fill us up! Prayer is the difference between being spiritually dynamic and spiritually dead; between being victorious over Satan and being victimized by him. We have been given prayer as a spiritual weapon, and using it properly can make a radical difference in the way we think and act. How easy it is for our words to simply be echoes from empty shells rather than the cries of a warrior for the mission and purposes of God! Let me share three ways to pray that make a powerful difference.

Pray According to God's Purpose

So much can be learned about God from what he asks us to pray. God makes it clear in the Word that we are to pray for strength (Psalm 22:19), wisdom (James 1:5), help (Mark 14:35), faith (Luke 22:32), perseverance (Luke 18:1), our enemies (Matthew 5:44), other disciples (John 17:6-26), and the lost (Matthew 9:38) among others. Just as we ask others to pray about the things that mean the most to us, God wants us to pray about the things that mean the most to him.

Recently, a brother named Mark who works as a computer programmer became very frustrated with the demands of his job. The 10-12 hour days spent in front of the computer left little opportunity to share his faith. After praying to God one day, he decided to "log on" and share his faith using the computer network asking, "Is there anybody out there who's searching for God?" Moments later, a man responded "Yes, I'm searching." That night he and his wife came to a Bible discussion and were both baptized two weeks later! When we pray for the purposes of God, our prayers exert mighty influence with him, and we are reminded that we truly serve a God that can do anything at any time!

Pray in Praise of God

Every prayer is aimed towards the throne of God, the Creator, the one that created billions of stars and millions of galaxies with mere words. Our God stands in greatness before us and *how we pray is as important as what we pray.*

Several months ago during a busy time in the ministry, I felt the need to get up early and pray the way Jesus prayed. I left the house at 4:30 a.m. in the dark, rural, wooded neighborhood where we lived.

As I began my prayer to "move God's heart" it was actually my heart that got moved. While walking through the darkened streets, I could see the eyes of small animals staring at me. The crackling early morning sounds that are usually taken for granted were somehow very alive with each step I took and caused my heart to break forth in praise. I couldn't help but think that Jesus felt this way as he walked up the dark hills to pray each morning. As I prayed and understood my need to depend on God, I felt stronger and incredibly resolved. I continued my early morning walks throughout the month, finding I was becoming more fearless than ever before. Not surprisingly, the church began to experience some of its greatest growth. The saying is so true, "He who has praised well has prayed well." When we pray in praise to God, he always makes a difference in our lives.

Pray for the Passion to Produce

"Ask the Lord of the harvest, therefore, to send out workers into the harvest field," said Jesus (Matthew 9:38). Not only was he reassuring the disciples that the LORD is the Lord of the Harvest, but he was also telling them that *it is God's will* that there *be* a harvest!

When I became a Christian I made the big mistake of offending my family the first time I went home. For the next three years no one in the family was interested in my faith or conviction. *No one* was willing to listen, and at times I wondered if God had a purpose for my family! I knew I had to pray to God to miraculously give them a change of heart. For the next 11 years I prayed the same prayer daily, asking God to permit each of my seven brothers and sisters to study the whole message of salvation and discipleship in their lifetime.

Now my mother, my brother, and three of my sisters have all been baptized as disciples! It was so exciting recently to have my mom at the church service and for our family to take up the entire first row! As Jesus prayed one of his final prayers for the world, his ultimate desire was for every word we speak to the world about God to produce fruit (John 17:20).

Our prayers are more than mere words. As disciples, we must understand how important prayer is in the eyes of God Almighty. Our lives will be transformed forever if we understand the kind of prayer that God honors and expects, for we will then understand the God whom we serve. We serve a God who is worthy of praise, a God who always provides, and a God whose passion is to harvest more souls. Pray like a warrior and make a difference in this world!

Prayer

O Lord, my God! The heavens and earth declare the wonders of your mighty hands. Lord, I praise you with my whole heart for your faithfulness, and this wondrous life of never-ending fellowship and closeness to you. For who in the heavens above can compare with the Lord Almighty? When I consider the works of your hands I stand in awe. When I look at your creation I am inspired, and my lips break forth with praise. Lord, keep me on my knees near your mighty throne, so that prayer will be the ongoing expression of my love and closeness to you.

You have brought me forth from darkness to fulfill your good purpose. Thank you that as a son my prayers can make a difference and exert mighty influence with you. You have given me the passion to produce and made me fruitful in the midst of your great assembly. Therefore, my heart is refreshed and rejoices in my God and Savior. Teach us to pray more powerfully, that we might be more effective workers in your kingdom and so that together we turn the world upside down in this generation! Through Jesus. Amen.

For Further Study:

Philippians 4:6-7
Matthew 6:9-13
1 Peter 3:12

31
Our Eyes Are on You

Brian and Caryn Homet

Then Jehoshaphat stood up in the assembly of Judah and Jerusalem at the temple of the Lord in the front of the new courtyard and said:

"O Lord, God of our fathers, are you not the God who is in heaven? You rule over all the kingdoms of the nations. Power and might are in your hand, and no one can withstand you. O our God, did you not drive out the inhabitants of this land before your people Israel and give it forever to the descendants of Abraham your friend?...we have no power to face this vast army that is attacking us. We do not know what to do, but our eyes are upon you" (2 Chronicles 20:5-7,12).

Romanian Adventure

Sunday, July 10, 1994. When the phone rang at 3:00 a.m., it was business as usual. On Thursday, Caryn and I had spent our first night as missionaries to Bucharest, Romania, entertaining our very curious, energetic and strong-willed 10-month-old daughter. Earlier she who had decided that flying on an airplane was too much fun a time to waste sleeping.

The following night the phone rang at midnight. The rest of our mission team, seven disciples from Boston, had finally made it to Bucharest—nine hours and two airports later than scheduled! I spent the next couple of hours dragging oversized and overpacked suitcases, duffel bags and backpacks up a flight of stairs, into a closet-sized elevator, up another eight floors, across a rooftop walkway, into another elevator and down seven more floors to help the sisters move into their apartment.

This was but a foreshadowing of the great adventure even simple tasks can be in the third world. Returning home, I was welcomed by a screaming daughter, the barking and howling of stray dogs claiming the night, and the constant whine of thirsty mosquitoes anxious to greet the new tenants. So why should a phone call at 3:00 a.m. on Sunday come as a surprise?

"Hello?" It was Randy McKean calling from Paris! It's always great to hear from Randy...but 3:00 a.m.? We were expecting Randy to arrive Monday to lead 50 disciples (our team plus 40 more from the churches in Berlin and Munich), in the evangelistic campaign. His son had fallen ill *en route* with appendicitis and would need an emergency operation. Randy would not be able to come until Friday afternoon; his wife, Kay, couldn't make it at all.

Through all our trials—delayed flights, sleepless nights, hot days, cold showers, the dogs, the mosquitoes—this thought had encouraged me: "No matter, the McKeans are coming!" Randy and Kay had taught us so much, raising us up to be leaders in Boston. Now, I thought, they would teach us from their years of experience starting and building churches on three continents. We would walk with two of the best, watch every step, cling to every word. But now the word was, "See you Friday!" *Friday?* Friday!

I felt my heart drop to the floor. Or maybe it was my stomach. Whatever it was, I had reached a limit. The news hit Caryn hard as well. To mark the moment (now 3:30 a.m.), the dogs outside our window went into a particularly frenzied round of barking.

Broken or Crushed

It was time to pray. Not just any prayer, but a Jehoshaphat prayer...a prayer of desperation, of deep-felt need for God. As I prayed on, it became clear that this was a prayer of surrender to God and his sovereignty. "O Lord, we do not know what to do, but our eyes are upon you." I realized that God had brought me to this breaking point, and I felt a great heaviness on my heart. "Jesus said to them '...he who falls on this stone will be broken to pieces, but he on whom it falls will be crushed'" (Matthew 21:42, 44). Broken or crushed—that was the choice. Get broken or get crushed—that was the reality. And so I prayed. The battle lines were drawn and Satan was trying to defend his stronghold from God's advancing troops. I not only prayed for victory, but for God to turn Satan's weapons against him. I prayed for God to glorify himself in an impossible situation and inspire the churches in Boston and Continental Europe. Caryn and I prayed for over 500 at our first service. I pledged to God that, no matter what came our way, we would not back down.

The week of our campaign had all the ingredients of a disaster: it rained most days, Romanian college students were taking their final exams and many others had left the city for summer vacations, we had trouble finding a translator for the first service and we had no Romanian speakers on the team! But nothing could steal our faith, found in prayer, that *God* had brought us here and *God* would somehow make it happen. Every morning, the 50 disciples bowed in prayer together and sang songs of praise and victory. At day's end, after hours and hours of evangelism, we prayed and praised some more. And God moved, bringing a total of 516 on Sunday! Five days later, Dragos was baptized—our first conversion! At this writing, we've seen 25 Romanians come into God's kingdom, and the church has tripled!

Leaving our family and friends, leading a church in a third world country, living in a foreign culture, learning a new language...the stones have never been larger in our lives then here in Romania. At times, we've felt the weight is more than we can bear. But we are thankful for the leaders who have taught us to be people of faith and people of prayer. We've learned that "brokenness and prayer" is not a decision for life, but a life of decisions. Again and again, we must see where we are without God and without prayer. The stones are heavy and rough, but God is moving them to shape us into his image. Broken or crushed? The difference is prayer.

Prayer

Lord, I need you right now. I always need you, but now I'm feeling it more than I have in a long time. Father, as I come before you in prayer, my heart is humbled. You, O Lord, created the heavens and the earth. You,

Father, formed man in your image and breathed life into him. You set the boundaries of time and space, of right and wrong, of life and death. When man rebelled against you and your laws, you raised up the faithful to win mighty victories in your name and for your honor. You sent your Son to earth in a mighty display of your love and your truth, and Satan fell like lightning. Nothing that opposes you can stand against you.

Father, I'm sorry I am so prideful. I'm sorry I think I know more than I know, that I think I can do more than I can do. Without you, I can do nothing. Without you, I am nothing. With you, nothing is impossible! Thank you for this reminder that you are God and I am yours.

God, I love you. Thank you for loving me—for giving me your light, your hope, your salvation, your name! I repent of my pride and my selfishness. I pledge to you a willing and grateful heart. My life is yours. Use my life to build your kingdom, however and wherever you choose. May our family shine with the light of Christ in this dark place. In Jesus' name, Amen!

FOR FURTHER STUDY:

Hebrews 11:1-19
2 Corinthians 4:7-18
Revelation 21:1-8

Epilogue
God Is Eager

Frank Kim, *Denver, Colorado*

> Then the disciples came to Jesus in private and asked, "Why couldn't we drive it out?"
>
> He replied, "Because you have so little faith. I tell you the truth, if you have faith as small as a mustard seed, you can say to this mountain, 'Move from here to there' and it will move. Nothing will be impossible for you" (Matthew 17:19-20).

It wasn't a question of effort. Jesus' disciples had left home and family, traveled through countless towns, pushed through thronging crowds, and had even helped many to come to faith. However, when they tried their best to heal this unfortunate boy—*they couldn't do it.* "Because you have so little faith."

Do you have faith? A timeless challenge, especially to disciples determined to realize the quest of evangelizing an entire planet in one generation. You see, if our efforts should end in failure, our ultimate downfall will not have been language or cultural barriers, financial difficulties, political repression or even persecution. The problem will have been, quite simply, a lack of faith.

Faith and prayer go hand in hand. Without faith, prayer becomes an empty mantra, a meaningless cadence rather than a blessing that brings you into the life-changing presence of the Almighty God. Without faith, prayer is a burden to be borne rather than a confident call upon our eager and powerful Father. Prayer is an area of our Christian life that often embodies guilt for the average Christian. For many, it has become an issue of "How long?" "How much?" "How loud?" The focus has become self-effort, and the result is boring and powerless. Ultimately, the point of prayer can never be *our* perseverance, *our* lengthiness or *our* volume. The focus must be God. Because if we truly knew God, we couldn't help but believe that such a God can and will work powerfully in our lives. That is faith, and that is the motive behind prayer.

As an Asian, I am thankful for the discipline and goal-oriented way in which I was raised. Living in Japan, however, I often see the negative aspects of intensively pushing children to excel in academic areas. Often there are tremendous insecurities linked to the belief that affection or reward is conditional upon success or effort.

Several years ago, my prayer life, as well as my entire outlook on my relationship with God, changed when I realized that this type of thinking had infiltrated my own relationship with God. I believed God could do anything. But I was not convinced that God *wanted* to bless me or my ministry. As a result, my prayer life and efforts in other areas became means by which I tried to convince God to bless me. If I prayed long enough, or fasted long enough, then God would have to answer. This "prove it" philosophy drove me to great efforts, but it also wore down my enthusiasm and drive. My faith was always wrapped up in worrying about whether I had done enough to earn God's blessing.

Reading through the Scriptures, however, I discovered a completely different attitude. I began to realize that God *wants* to bless us—abundantly and beyond our belief. (See Matthew 7:7-11, Ephesians 3:14-21). Most importantly, God doesn't simply expect us to be fruitful and evangelize the world. He *wants* to make us fruitful, and he is constantly working to enable his kingdom to realize that dream—his dream. God wants to save the lost; he loves people around you and in your city more than you do! I don't need to convince God to work...I can have deep conviction that he is already powerfully working to strengthen me and my ministry to be abundantly fruitful. The result? More desire, more enthusiasm, more intensity than ever, because I am convinced that God will bring about the ultimate victory (2 Samuel 22).

Consider these three thoughts as you strive to pray with greater faith:

- God *can* do it: God is almighty.

- God *wants* to do it: Remember his heart's desire—that people are saved.

- God *will* do it: Amen!

APPENDIX

Take a pen and build on paper a prayer that reasons with God. Then fall on your knees and start to pray to your Heavenly Father, our Almighty God. Remember to be completely humble.

Prayer "Help Me to Be Fruitful"

Reason 1: _____

Reason 2: _____

Reason 3: _____

Prayer: Help Me to Change (be specific):

Reason 1: _____

Reason 2: _____

Reason 3: _____

Prayer: Help Me to Fulfill My Kingdom Dreams

Dream 1: _____

Reason 1: _____

Reason 2: _____

Reason 3: _____

Dream 2: _____

Reason 1: _____

Reason 2: _____

Reason 3: _____

Who Are We?

Illumination Publishers International (IP Books) began publishing in 2003. It was begun by Toney C. Mulhollan and is affiliated with churches committed to following the Bible and making disciples of all nations. It publishes and distributes materials that honor God, lift up Jesus Christ and show how his message practically applies to all areas of life. We have a deep conviction that no one changes life like Jesus and that the implementation of his teaching will revolutionize any life, any marriage, any family, and any single.

Since our begining we have published over 224 books and with the acquisition of Discipleship Publications International (DPI) several years ago, we now have over 330 titles and thousands of audio lessons and teaching series. More than three million volumes have been printed, and our works have been translated into more than a dozen languages.

You can find us at www.ipibooks.com. Download our IPI App for easy ordering. We appreciate the thousands of comments we have received from readers so keep them coming.

www.ipibooks.com

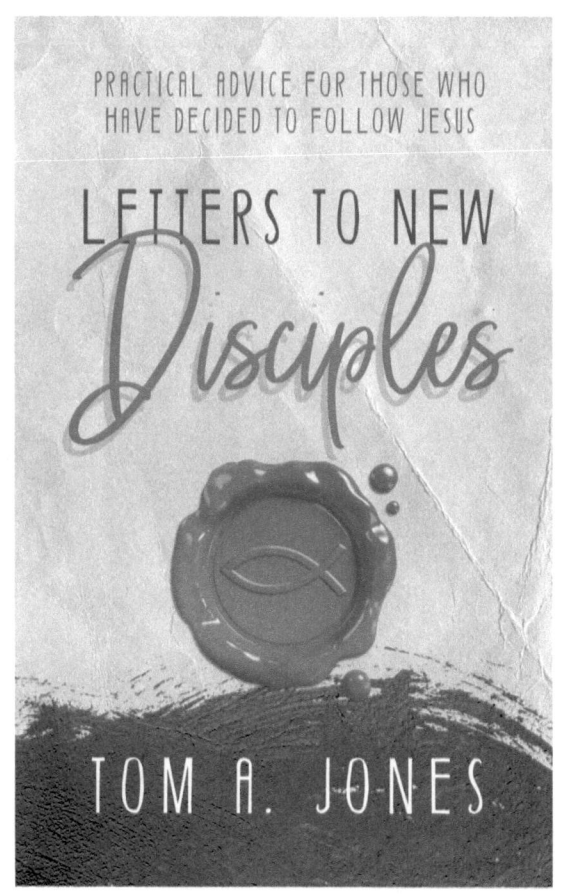

PRACTICAL ADVICE FOR THOSE WHO
HAVE DECIDED TO FOLLOW JESUS

LETTERS TO NEW
Disciples

TOM A. JONES

Book by Tom A. Jones

www.ipibooks.com